WITHDRAWN

Memoirs of a Malayan Family

11

NAKHODA MUDDA

MEMOIRS

OF A

MALAYAN FAMILY,

WRITTEN BY THEMSELVES.

MEMOIRS

OF A

MALAYAN FAMILY,

WRITTEN BY THEMSELVES,

AND

TRANSLATED FROM THE ORIGINAL

BY

W. MARSDEN, F.R.S.

&c. &c.

LONDON:
PRINTED FOR THE ORIENTAL TRANSLATION FUND.
SOLD BY
J. MURRAY, ALBEMARLE STREET;
AND
PARBURY, ALLEN & CO., LEADENHALL STREET.

1830.

JOHNSON REPRINT CORPORATION   JOHNSON REPRINT COMPANY LTD.
111 Fifth Avenue, New York, N.Y. 10003   Berkeley Square House, London, W. 1

DS
646.13
N35
1968

First reprinting, 1968, Johnson Reprint Corporation
Printed in the United States of America

INTRODUCTION.

THE Malayan biographical tract of which the following is a translation, appears to have been chiefly drawn up, from time to time as the circumstances occurred, by the principal member of the family whose history it relates, and subsequently added to and finally arranged by one of his younger sons, whose name of *'La-uddīn* is found at the conclusion of the manuscript. The date of it he has neglected to insert; but the omission is supplied, with sufficient accuracy, by his mentioning the name of the English gentleman at whose desire the transcript was made, and who is known to have been Chief of the district in which the writer had taken up his abode, about the year 1788. A deficiency, however, of a more serious kind exists, in there not being any statements throughout the manuscript, of the years in which the several occurrences took place, although the intervals of time between each are carefully marked.

marked. But this also is remedied in great measure by the incidental notice of some public transactions,* which enable us to ascertain that the most eventful period of the narrative was comprised between the years 1756 and 1766, when Mr. Carter, whose protection the family sought, was relieved in the government of Bencoolen.

The memoirs, although without any pretension to political or literary importance, are by no means destitute of interest; but their principal merit is that of exhibiting a genuine picture, by a native hand, of Malayan manners and dispositions, more forcibly, and, it may be said, more dramatically represented, than they could be drawn by the pencil of any stranger. They have also the recommendation of affording a specimen of simple narrative; a style of which some writers have thought the Malays incapable, and which is certainly rare in comparison with the romantic and extravagant tales so prevalent amongst these and other eastern people. Nor should we be too fastidious on the subject of their humble attempts at biography,

* Particularly the capture of the English settlements in Sumatra by a French squadron under the Comte d'Estaing, in April 1760, and their re-occupation in the following year.

graphy, when we reflect on the small degree of historical interest that belongs to some of our own most popular works of the same class.

The manuscript was sent to England in the year 1791, and not long afterwards received the dress in which it now appears, whilst the translator was employed in compiling a dictionary of the Malayan language. Its having remained so long unattended to since that period, is to be attributed to various causes, some of a personal and others of a public nature. Among the latter was the consideration, more especially, that the subject-matter of the memoirs being so nearly connected with the disagreements between the English and Dutch East-India Companies, or their respective governments abroad, on the grounds, or pretences of rights infringed, enemies countenanced, and other grievances, they could not have been published at the time without the hazard of giving umbrage to the one party or the other; but the circumstances being since entirely changed; the persons implicated in the transactions, both Europeans and Malays, having long ceased to exist; the rules of conduct towards the country powers being established on a more enlightened policy than

formerly

formerly prevailed; and every pretext for future national differences being removed by the treaty of 1824,* there no longer appears to be any sufficient motive for suppressing a recital (true in substance, however partially coloured) that may serve as an useful warning to all persons who, in those countries, are placed in situations of discretionary control, to be just, as well as cautious in their proceedings with a spirited and adventurous race of people, who have strong feelings of independence, are impatient of injury, jealous of insult, and who consider the indulgence of revenge as a duty at least, if not a virtue.

* By this treaty England consented to withdraw its establishments, and to relinquish in favour of the Netherlands, all right to settle or maintain factories in the island of Sumatra; the latter power agreeing, on its part, to renounce a claim to territorial rights over the small island of *Singapore,* on which, as an unoccupied spot, a settlement had been recently formed by the English; and also to give up its factories on the continent of India.

MEMOIRS

OF A

MALAYAN FAMILY.

This narrative, which contains a full detail of events that took place at the period of the Dutch (East-India) Company's taking measures for establishing a settlement at *Samangka*,* is transcribed for the information of the (English) resident (chief) of *Laye*,† who has expressed

---

* The name of a district in the *Lampōng* country, as well as of a large bay near the western entrance of the Straits of Sunda, on the Sumatran side, otherwise called by the Dutch, Keyser's Bay. It does not appear from the maps that the name of *Samangka* was applied to any particular town; nor, especially, is it found in a survey made of the bay by direction of the late Sir Stamford Raffles, or in his excellent map of Sumatra recently published. There is reason, however, to believe that the place called *Birni* or *Birné* at its further extremity, is that which was occupied by this family and other Malays, and where the Dutch hoisted their flag; for in a sketch made at the time by Captain Thomas Forrest, and published in Dalrymple's Collection, it is the only spot where he has marked a town; and it cannot be supposed that he would have omitted the place where he procured refreshments, and lay (as will appear) ten days at anchor. Nor is it extraordinary that in the course of this narrative the well-known name of the bay should be employed instead of that belonging to an obscure river at the mouth of which the Malays had fixed themselves.

† A residency or settlement on the south-western coast of Sumatra, about thirty miles from Bencoolen, of which Mr. B. Hunnings was then chief.

expressed a wish to be made acquainted with the circumstances.

A Malay, a native of *Bāyang** in the kingdom of *Menangkabau*,† who was distinguished by the appellation of *Nakhoda Makūta*, undertook a trading voyage to Java, and continued for some time to navigate from one port to another of that country. Visiting afterwards an island called *Karimāta*, situated between *Pasīr* and *Banjar*,‡ which he found to be the resort of a considerable number of Malays, who were drawn thither, as well for its being suited to the purposes of commerce, as on account of gold mines at that time worked by the natives; and observing it to be a place where the people lived undisturbed in their industrious pursuits, he formed the resolution of making it his future residence, and accordingly took to himself a wife. He had not, however, been settled there more than three years, when a fleet (of praws) from the *Būgis* country (Celebes), commanded by *Panglima Tuāsah*, made its appearance and commenced hostilities; the reputed wealth of the inhabitants holding out a strong temptation for plunder. The attacks were resisted during the space of a month, but the invaders continually receiving fresh succours at length

* A place not many miles to the south-east of *Padang*, on the western coast of Sumatra.

† For an account of this ancient, and probably original Malayan kingdom, see the History of Sumatra, p. 332.

‡ Ports of Borneo; but the situation here described applies rather to *Pŭlo Lāut* than to *Karimāta*, which lies on the western or opposite side of the great island.

length prevailed, and the people on shore were reduced to the necessity of saving themselves by flight in the best manner they could. Some made their escape in praws, and some in sampans (canoes), whilst others fled on foot (to the interior of the island). *Nakhoda Makūta* embarked in a praw, and sailing at night, unobserved by the enemy, reached in safety a place named *Tāyan*, in the country of *Banjar* (in Borneo).

About a year after his arrival, his wife bore him a son, to whom he gave the name of *Inchi Tāyan*. When the child had attained its third year, he began to reflect on the expediency of changing his residence; from the consideration that in the event of his own death, an infant of that tender age, without a father or relatives, would be exposed to danger. Influenced by this motive he took measures for building a praw, for which he provided a cargo as soon as she was ready for sea, and when a fortunate hour presented itself, he set sail, with his family and household, for a trading voyage to the country of *Lampōng*.* The space of time employed in the voyage is not mentioned, but he disembarked at a place called *Piābōng*,† where he found a number of Malays living under the jurisdiction of a *pañgeran* (native chief), who received his title of *Pañgeran Surabawa* from the sultan of *Bantam* (in Java). Upon this

---

* A district that embraces the southern extremity of Sumatra; but the name is particularly applied to a bay within the Straits of Sunda, and near to that of *Samangka*.

† An inconsiderable place in *Lampōng* Bay.

this person he waited, to pay his respects, and recounted to him the events of his life, particularly the circumstances attending his flight from *Karimāta*. The chief appeared to feel much concern at the recital, and said to him, " *Nakhoda*,* you will do wisely to fix your " abode in my country, and cease to lead a wandering " life. Reflect that you are now advanced in years; but " if your inclination be still to employ yourself in the " pursuit of gain, there is ample scope for trade between " this place and Bantam." *Makūta* assented to this proposal, and when their conversation was at an end, returned to his vessel for the purpose of landing her cargo. This being effected, he hauled her on shore and laid her up. His next object was to build a house near the mouth of *Piābōng* river, where he established himself as a trader. Many people, as well *Lampōngs* as Malays, resorted to him for the purchase of his goods; but even though the purpose of their visit should be merely to converse and ask questions, he never failed to answer them with mildness in his words and complacency in his manner. His dealings were open and candid, he was above all dishonourable arts, and he avoided everything that might lead to jealousy or dispute with the inhabitants. The consequence of which prudent conduct was, that during the whole period of his living among them he never ceased to experience their good will.

His

---

* A Persian term adopted by the Malays, denoting a person who is at the same time navigator and owner of a trading vessel; a condition of much respectability amongst these commercial people.

His son *Tāyan* being now of sufficient age, he had him taught to repeat the formularies of religion, and afterwards to write. Thus instructed he was sent to visit several countries, the names of which have not been recorded. Seven years were employed in this manner; at the expiration of which he returned to reside at *Piābōng*. By this time the father was far advanced in years;. living respected by the *pañgeran*, beloved by the Malays, and regarded as their chief by all the merchants established there. He resolved that his son should not thence-forward undertake any long voyage. " Con-
" tent yourself," he said to him, " with making trips " between this port and *Bantam*,whither you may convey " cargoes of pepper; and even if you should effect only " one trip in the season, you may still make it answer, by " employing yourself during the intervals, with the aid " of a few domestics, in cultivating a rice plantation."

The value of pepper in this part of the country, if the advances of money are made in the preceding year, that is, six months before, is six (Spanish) dollars for the *bahar* (five hundred weight), or seven dollars, if the purchase be made at the place of weighing for money paid down. Such are the established rates in all parts of *Lampōng*, within the jurisdiction of the sultan. Now this pepper, when safely transported to Bantam, is resold to the sultan for twelve dollars the *bahar*; and be the quantity what it may, he never fails to take it off. By him it is again disposed of to the Dutch Company at twenty dollars, according to an agreement that has long subsisted

subsisted between them.* The Company cannot purchase it in the first instance from the chiefs of the country, nor from the Malay traders, without the consent of the sultan, and if these should be detected in the sale of it, they would become liable to capital punishment; the pepper having ever been considered as at the exclusive disposal of the prince.

In compliance with the wishes of his father, *Tāyan* confined himself to the short navigation pointed out to him. About twelve months after this time his name of manhood was bestowed upon him,† and from thenceforwards he was distinguished by the appellation of *Nakhoda Mūda*.

When he had been engaged for the space of four or five years in the business of conveying pepper to Bantam, it happened that his father was seized with a dangerous illness, and upon being called to his presence, the latter thus addressed his son: " O my child, the " fruit of my heart and light of my eyes, preserve as a " sacred deposit the advice that I now give you. When " the decree of the Almighty shall have been fulfilled with " respect to me, and by my death you shall have become " your own master, avoid carefully to contract debts. If " your capital should be insufficient for your employing " it in mercantile adventures, cut timber in the woods,
" dispose

* The price paid to the planters, at that period, by the English Company, was fifteen dollars the *bahar*, exclusive of the customary allowances or duties to the chiefs.

† For an explanation of this cognomen or titular name, termed *galar*, see Hist. of Sumatra, p. 285.

"dispose of it, and raise a capital; catch fish in the sea, "dispose of them, and raise a capital; but do not dare "to run in debt, either to the sultan, the Company, or "any individual. Observe this injunction, my dear son!" Shortly after pronouncing these words, *Nakhoda Makūta* breathed his last, in the country of *Piābōng*. The commands he gave were listened to with attention by *Nakhoda Mūda*, who treasured them up in his heart and never swerved from them.

About three years after this event he married, according to the mode termed *semanda*,* a person from *Samangka*, the daughter of *Nakhoda Padūka*, who at his death left only this child, whose name was *Radin Mantri*. Her the relations bestowed in marriage on *Nakhoda Mūda* of *Piābōng*. Two years afterwards he made a trading voyage to *Samangka*, and upon his return asked his wife whether she felt a strong attachment to her own country, as in that case he should make no difficulty in gratifying her wishes by removing thither. "Nothing," she replied, "could be more agreeable to me than to "revisit *Samangka*, and especially as I have there some "plantations of coco-nut and other fruit-trees, which I "inherited from my family, and have left behind me." Upon this he embarked with his wife and all his household, in a praw, and removed to that place, where, upon his arrival he built a house. The produce of pepper

in

---

* In this, the proper Malayan mode, as distinguished from those in use amongst the country people, the rights of the two parties are reciprocal. See Hist. of Sumatra, p. 226.

in the country being considerable, he found full employment every season in transporting the article to Bantam; where also he married a wife. At this time his family at *Samangka* consisted of nine children, three daughters and six sons. The eldest of all was named *Inchī Pīsang*, the next, *Inchī Tenūn* (daughters), then a boy named *Wasub*; the next was born at Bantam, and named *Wasal*; then again at *Samangka*, one named *Bantan*, and another named *'La-uddīn*; then the third daughter, named *Brīsih*, and *Muhammed* and *Raff-uddīn*, (sons); making in the whole ten children, (including the one born at *Bantam*). Besides these were three which he had by concubines; one, a boy, named *Rabū*, and two girls named *Si-Rami* and *Si-Khamis*. From the period of his removal to *Samangka*, the number of Malayan settlers there continually increased.

Beyond the hills that lie inland of this place, there lived a people known by the appellation of *Abūng*, who occupied ten villages. This singular custom prevailed among them, that when their young men proposed to marry, they were required to undergo a year's probation before their offers were accepted. In order to fulfil this, they formed parties, to the number perhaps of ten persons, each of whom armed himself with a spear, a sword, and a kris, and thus equipped they set out on an expedition. Their provisions were three (gallon) measures of rice, with as much sugar as each man chose to provide; the use of this last article being to make a composition with decayed wood, on which to subsist, should

should their rice be expended. The object of these enterprises was to cut off the heads of such persons as they should encounter on the road; and in this pursuit they were sometimes led as far as the sea-coast, in the neighbourhood of *Samangka*. Scarcely a month passed without some of the inhabitants losing their lives, whose bodies were afterwards found headless in the woods; and when there was occasion to visit the rice plantations or fell timber, unless four or five persons associated for defence, they dared not to venture into the country, from the dread entertained of these *Abūng* men.*

As soon as the invading party met with success in obtaining heads, they returned homeward. In the mean time their countrymen, expecting their approach, prepared coco-nut shells filled with milk, and placed in the paths through which they must pass to their respective villages. Such of the youths as were provided with trophies passed on to their houses, escorted by a numerous band of young women who met them on the road, and with every demonstration of joy, shewed their willingness to become the wives of the fortunate adventurers. Those, on the contrary, who returned empty-handed, were deterred by shame from entering the villages, when they perceived the ranges of coco-nut shells filled with milk; because the ceremony implied that they were to be

* Mention is made of this savage tribe in the Hist. of Sumatra, originally published in 1783, several years before these memoirs were brought to England.

be looked upon and fed as dogs:* and it sometimes happened that to the hour of their death, these never revisited their homes. The use to which the sculls were subsequently applied, was this. The young man who was about to marry put into his trophy some gold or silver, in order to present it to the parent of his intended wife; and when the nuptial ceremony was to be performed, the scull was filled with toddy of the palm tree, of which the bride and bridegroom alternately drank. The rites were then complete; whereas if this were neglected, such an imperfect marriage would be regarded only as a state of concubinage, and the woman would not receive the respect paid to a lawful wife. Such were the customs of the *Abūng* people, who lived beyond the hills of *Samangka*.†

Nakhoda Mūda reflecting on these circumstances, said
to

* The natives of the Malay islands neither drink milk nor make butter. The same is said of the Chinese.

† This story, which has much the air of romance, might, with perfect consistency, be reduced to simple matter of fact. The people of the hills and those of the lower country were (as very commonly happens) in a state of continual and inveterate hostility, retaliating as opportunities offered, and giving no quarter. Those of the hills, though strong in their natural defences, were inferior to the others in point of numbers and means of offence. The object of their policy must therefore have been to surprise stragglers, and their young men were incited to shew their activity and skill in this species of warfare, by the most effectual encouragement that could be held out to them; that of bestowing their young women on those, in preference, who most distinguished themselves. Of their comparative merit the only ostensible proof was the number of heads brought back with them; and the ignomy attendant on the want of success (however accidental), has nothing in it of an extraordinary character.

to himself, " As long as the *Abūng* people remain un-
" subdued, the inhabitants of this place must always
" be exposed to danger; and it is intolerable that a
" person cannot venture to walk into the country alone."
Under these impressions he proceeded to consult with
Kiria Minjan, agent for the sultan of *Bantam* at *Samangka*, about the expediency of making an attack upon
their villages. *Kiria* agreed with him in opinion, and
proposed that they should assemble their respective dependants; giving notice of their design to the chiefs
of the country. These chiefs were four *pañgerans*;
namely, *Wei Ratna* of *Beniawang*, whose jurisdiction
comprehended twenty *kampongs* (or palisadoed villages);
Laūt Darasanta of *Bībū Lūñgū*, who had eighteen
villages; *Jaya Kasūma* of *Padang Rata*, who had
ten, and *Wei Samangkal* of *Samawang*, whose dependants were numerous and occupied thirteen villages.
All these chiefs were summoned, and in about five days
they assembled at *Samangka* to discuss the proposed
measures; when *Kiria Minjan* thus addressed them:
" The subject on which *Nakhoda Mūda* and myself
" have called you together is, the expediency, as it
" appears to our judgments, of conquering the *Abūng*
" people, in order that the inhabitants of this country
" may be relieved from apprehension and enabled to
" attend to their pepper and rice plantations, which, as
" we are informed, they cannot do at present without
" imminent risk, should they venture to go singly: and
" for this state of things, there seems to be no other
" remedy.

"remedy." The *pañgerans* unanimously replied: "The "circumstances, *Kiria Minjan*, are as you represent, "and we perfectly concur with you in opinion as to "the necessity of the war; but for our parts we are "entirely unprovided with the proper arms, such as "pieces of ordnance and musquets. Our weapons are "no other than long lances, which must prove exceed- "ingly inconvenient in a country where hills are to be "continually ascended and descended."*—" No diffi- "culties," said *Nakhoda Mūda*, " need to be made "respecting arms. Such of the dependants of the "country chiefs as accompany me, may be provided "with the common short lances; the long ones being "useless." He was appointed sole leader of the expe- dition; nor was it accompanied either by *Kiria Minjan* or by any of the *pañgerans* in person. The force em- ployed consisted of about four hundred men, of whom eighty carried musquets; the remainder being armed in a variety of modes. After spending three days in making their way through uninhabited forests, they approached the neighbourhood of the *Abūng* villages. A council of war being now held, *Nakhoda Mūda* gave orders that the people belonging to the country chiefs should remain where they were, for the present, whilst he advanced with those who were armed with musquets; but that as soon as they should hear the report of a gun, they were to hasten immediately to the spot. Marching close

---

* These very long lances are described in the Hist. of Sumatra, as being borne by three men. See p. 261 of early editions, or 297 of new.

close up to one of the villages, named *Minjang*, he ordered a shot to be fired into it, and then entered with his men: but they found it empty; having been abandoned by the inhabitants, who had fled in various directions. The remainder of the force now came up, and fell to plundering such effects as were left in the houses. Inquiry was then made of persons acquainted with the country, whether the other villages of these people were far distant from thence, and upon being informed to the contrary, *Nakhoda Mūda*, immediately proceeded against them with all his followers. The particular names of these places are not mentioned, but of the ten not one remained untaken, and by order of the commander the houses were burnt to the ground. Two months were employed in searching for the fugitives, scarcely any of whom could be discovered. Such as they happened to fall in with were hunted like deer in the forest; none attempting to make resistance, so much were they terrified by the report of fire-arms; nothing of the kind having ever been heard among them, either in the course of their own lives or from the days of their forefathers. In all this destruction of villages, however, not more than four of the *Abūng* people were killed by the musquetry; and of the four hundred who accompanied *Nakhoda Mūda*, not one man lost his life, and only one was wounded in the foot by a *ranjau*.* Since this event nothing has been certainly known

* These are small, sharpened stakes of bamboo, stuck in the ground to annoy a pursuing, barefooted enemy.

known of these fugitives, but it was reported that they had fled as far as the sea, on the opposite side of the island, and were settled near *Palembang*. *Nakhoda Mūda* and his army returned to *Samangka*, where they were met by *Kiria* and the *pañgerans*, and eagerly questioned respecting the circumstances of their campaign; of which a complete detail was afforded. Being now satisfied of the entire dispersion of the *Abūng* people, those of *Samangka* were relieved from further apprehension. After four or five days had been spent in festivities and rejoicing in the town, the country chiefs returned to their respective villages with hearts quite at ease.

Half a year had elapsed from the time of this transaction, when *Nakhoda Mūda* made a voyage to *Bantam* with a cargo of pepper. Upon his arrival he waited on the principal minister of the sultan and depositary of his confidence in all business, of whatever nature, within his realm, whose title was *Pañgeran Kasūma Niñgrat*. Upon entering the house, he sat down (respectfully) in the presence of the minister, who, when he perceived him, said; " When did *Nakhoda Mūda* arrive? What " cargo has he brought? What news was stirring at " *Samangka* when he left it?"—" My lord *pañgeran*," replied he, " I have brought nothing besides pepper; " being the only produce of the country. Of this I " have one hundred *bahars* (about thirty tons). As to " news there was none, excepting what relates to a " certain people beyond the hills, who had no king nor
" were

" were under any certain government; belonging neither
" to his highness the sultan of *Bantam*, nor to the
" sultan of *Palembang*, nor to any other power. So
" great was the terror they inspired, that when any of
" them were known to approach the coast, the inhabi-
" tants of *Samangka* dared not to venture into the
" country, from the dread of being murdered. This
" caused the chiefs to resolve upon attacking their
" villages, and to appoint me to proceed thither at the
" head of their dependants; on which occasion the
" villages were all destroyed, to the number of ten." The
minister expressed himself to be extremely gratified by
this intelligence, and *Nakhoda Mūda*, after some further
conversation, took his leave, to return to his vessel.

As soon as the landing of his cargo was effected, an
officer on the part of the sultan, and another on the part
of the Dutch Company, attended to receive it. When
weighed, the amount was paid in dollars, which he laid
out in goods for the *Samangka* market. His returning
cargo being ready, he again waited on the minister, to
signify his intention of departing. " *Nakhoda Mūda*,"
said he, " as your residence is at *Samangka*, it is expe-
" dient that you should be in a capacity of rendering
" service to the sultan, in your district, which is far
" removed from the seat of government. Should any
" disputes, or actual hostilities take place amongst the
" *pañgerans* or *proatins* (heads of villages), be it your
" duty, in conjunction with *Kiria Minjan* (the agent),
" to inquire into the causes of their difference, and,

" provided

"provided that no lives have been lost, to adjust the "affair, judicially, on the spot: but in the event of any "persons being killed, the *proatīns* must be sent over to "*Bantam*, and the particulars of the affray communi- "cated to me in writing. Moreover, when persons sent "from me and commissioned by the sultan, arrive at "*Samangka* for the purpose of making a survey of the "pepper plantations, do you, *Nakhoda Mūda*, accom- "pany them in the business. These, you must be "aware, are not my private suggestions, but the com- "mands of the sultan, which I have his directions to "make known to you."—" The performance of what "your Excellency requires," replied *Nakhoda Mūda*, "would not be attended with more trouble than what I "should willingly undertake; but I have doubts of the "appointment being satisfactory to the chiefs of the "country; seeing that I am no more than a settler in "the place, as is well known to your Excellency."— "All persons who dwell at *Samangka*," the minister observed, " are equally to be considered as settlers, and "as continuing to reside there under the sultan's licence; "nor can any one of them pretend to exercise power or "will, otherwise than through the sultan, to whom the "country has belonged from early times, unto the pre- "sent hour." To this, *Nakhoda Mūda* returned no further answer, but only took leave, preparatory to his departure; on which occasion the minister invested him with a complete dress, such as the *proatīns* in the dominions of the sultan of *Bantam* are accustomed to wear.

wear. Upon going down to the port, he waited on the Fiscal (Dutch officer of the customs), in order to procure a sea-pass for *Samangka*, and as soon as that was made out, he set sail, and performed the voyage in a short time.

About six months after his return a boat arrived from *Bantam* having on board two officers, who came, by the sultan's orders, to make a survey of the plantations belonging to every village, and brought direction to *Nakhoda Mūda* and *Kiria Minjan* to proceed along with them. They accordingly set out together, and in the progress of the survey (or circuit of inspection), the principal officer thus addressed the respective *proatins*: " It is by the command of his highness the sultan that " *Nakhoda Mūda*, in conjunction with *Kiria Minjan*, " accompanies us on this duty: you are not therefore to " feel any jealousy towards him for what he does in obe-" dience to those commands. If any difference should " hereafter arise between one *proatin* and another, or " even between the *pañgerans*, these two persons are " appointed by the sultan to decide upon it, and you " are required to abide by their decision. Such, be it " known to all whom it may concern, is the pleasure of " the sultan." In two months the business of the survey was completed, when the party returned to the town, and the boat (with the two officers) sailed for *Bantam*, carrying a small quantity of pepper from each of the country chiefs, as a complimentary tribute to his highness.

The

The Malayan town at *Samangka* continually increased in its population. There were about fifty praws belonging to the place, navigated by Malays, and employed in the transport of pepper. These were obliged to take out passes for their voyage from *Nakhoda Mūda*, and to produce them on their arrival at *Bantam*. In this manner he advanced in personal consequence, and rose in the esteem of the inhabitants of the place. The native *Lampōngs*, the Javans, and the Malays, were equally attached to him.

It happened that about this time a war broke out in the country of *Bantam*, between the sultan and the people of the hills. The leader of these insurgents was named *Rātū Bagus Būang*, a man of an active mind and of desperate resolution, whom none amongst the hill-chiefs dared to oppose, and whose word they implicitly followed. Under him they collected in a body to make an attack on the capital, and soon obtained possession of all the smaller towns in the neighbourhood. Even within the city itself, those persons who were not in immediate connexion with the court, were in general inclined to the party of *Rātū Bagus*. The only places of consequence that remained untaken, were three forts; one belonging to the sultan, named *Gadong Intan*, and two belonging to the Dutch, called *Pitchī* (?) and *Karang Antu*; the garrisons of which held out. The sultan, however, received occasional assistance from *Batavia*, and the war was carried on for the space of about two years; the insurgents being induced to maintain it with such

such obstinacy, by the prospect which *Rātū Bagus* held out to them, that in the event of his getting possession of the city, they would be relieved from all future control, either on the part of the sultan or of the Company. Endowed in an eminent degree with the art of working upon the minds of men, he led them in this manner to promote his designs, and to disregard the consequences of such proceedings.

Upon *Kirīa Minjan's* receiving the intelligence of the city of *Bantam* being attacked and of the probability of its capture, he immediately left *Samangka*, in order to join the party of *Rātū Bagus*, being himself a hill-man of the *Bantam* country. As soon as he was admitted to his presence, and made the customary obeisance, the *Rātū** inquired, " from whence does this man come?"— " He is," said the officers in attendance, " *Kirīa Minjan*, " who for some time past has had the management of " the *Samangka* country under the orders of the sultan, " and is arrived to pay his compliments to your high- " ness, in consequence of his learning that you are " making preparation to effect the conquest of the " city."—" Your slave," said *Kirīa*, " comes to express " his readiness to submit to the will of your highness, " and no longer acknowledges allegiance to the sultan."— " Are there," inquired the *Rātū*, " any Malays settled " at *Samangka?*"—" There are many, please your " highness, who are established there for the purposes of
" commerce;

---

* *Rātū* is a title of rank, denoting a feudal prince.

" commerce; perhaps two hundred and fifty men capable
" of bearing arms; and their chief is named *Nakhoda*
" *Mūda.*"—" Such being the case," said the *Rātū,* " do
" you return directly to *Samangka,* and bring hither to
" me all those Malays."—" But how am I to act,"
answered *Kiria,* " if they do not shew a willingness
" to obey your highness's commands by accompanying
" me?"—" If all should not be disposed to come, bring
" with you at least one hundred and fifty: by fair means,
" if they are submissive, or otherwise by force; but at
" all events bring them hither; and should any spirit of
" resistance be manifested, take off the head of their
" chief, and let it be conveyed to me."

After this conversation *Kiria* embarked from a place named *Kwāla Charingan,* for *Samangka,* being provided with two large boats, of the sort called *panchālang.* Upon his arrival, he repaired to the residence of *pangeran Wei Ratna* of *Beniāwang,* whom he thus addressed: " I am come hither, *pangeran,* by the orders
" of *Rātū Bagus Būang,* to make a progress through
" the country of *Lampōng,* and ascertain who amongst
" the chiefs are disposed to yield obedience to him as
" their sovereign, and who are not; it having become
" certain that he must soon render himself master of the
" city of *Bantam.* My reason for applying to you in
" the first instance is, that I consider you to be the
" principal person, in rank and consequence, of this
" country."—" If it were indeed certain," replied the *pangeran,* " that *Bantam* must submit to *Rātū Bagus,*
" there

" there would be no room for hesitation, because who-
" ever is king of that place is entitled to our allegiance:
" I hope that what I say does not give dissatisfaction."
" What is your opinion," said *Kirìa*, " with regard to
" the Malays who are settled here? Do you suppose
" them inclined to attach themselves to the cause of the
" *Rātū*, or the contrary? My reason for the inquiry is,
" that I have his instructions to cause all those Malays
" to join him; by fair means, if they are so disposed;
" or if not, by force."

It happened that this conversation was overheard by a person named *Radīn Sapang*, who was particularly attached to *Nakhoda Mūda*, and who immediately communicated to him the purport of it. Upon receiving the information, the latter called a meeting of all the *nakhodas* (masters and owners of trading praws) that were then in the Malayan town *(kampong malāyū)*. Being assembled at his house, he addressed them in the following words: " In what light, my brethren and
" fellow-traders, are you disposed to view the commis-
" sion brought by *Kirìa Minjan* from *Rātū Bagus*, for
" transporting us all to *Bantam?* If we shew a disin-
" clination to join in his measures, he will assuredly
" proceed to hostilities against us. Such is the in-
" formation communicated to me by *Radīn Sapang*.
" What, my brethren, should be resolved upon under
" these circumstances? Our decision must be instantly
" made; for at this moment *Kirìa Minjan* is at the
" village of *pungeran Wei Ratna*, collecting a force to
" march

" march this way." Of the traders who met together on this occasion some advised it, as the more prudent course, to accede to what should be proposed by the agent of the *Rātū;* whilst others maintained a contrary opinion; and there was no consistency in their deliberations. At length an elderly person named *Nakhoda Malim*, who came from *Kampar* (on the north-eastern coast of *Sumatra*), suggested, that since so much uncertainty prevailed amongst them, it would be expedient to refer the matter back to *Nakhoda Mūda*, and to request the aid of his counsel. This reference being approved of by the others, and his sentiments being desired accordingly, he said to them: " In my humble
" opinion, so long as the sultan of *Bantam* remains un-
" subdued, and the Dutch Company continues to exist
" at *Batavia*, it would be unwise in us to embrace
" the party of *Rātū Bagus Būang.* With regard to
" *Kiria*, if he shall judge it proper to advance towards
" us, I think it will be more advisable to resist him
" by open force, than to be led away by any pro-
" posals; as I am fully persuaded that *Bantam* will
" not be taken by his master, however brave he may be,
" so long as the sultan is furnished with succours from
" *Batavia.* Thus you have my counsel."—" This being
" the decision," said they, " no time should be lost; let
" each man of us get ready his arms, and let us proceed
" to occupy situations where we can most advantageously
" make a stand and oppose the enemy."

Nakhoda Mūda took measures for fitting out two
praws;

praws; which were well provided with arms and ammunition, and each had two experienced persons on board, who were instructed to lie off the mouth of the river for the purpose of intercepting *Kiria Minjan's* boats, in the event of his attempting to enter with them. The crews were all chosen men, and *Nakhoda Malim*, to whom the service was intrusted, had acquired much experience in naval warfare, from having been heretofore employed against the *Bājū* people.* As soon as this business had been arranged, he dispatched a small vessel to *Bantam*, with a letter to the sultan and another to the Dutch governor (chief or resident), Mynheer Sambirik,† acquainting them that an agent from *Rātū Bagus* had arrived at *Samangka*, for the purpose of securing that country for his master; that all the native chiefs were intimidated by him, but that the Malays, on the contrary, had shewn no disposition to submit to his (usurped) authority. Such was the purport of these letters, which he committed to the charge of a person named *Nakhoda Tangah*, who likewise carried a present to the sultan, of dried fish, rice, and ripe betel-nut, and to the Dutch governor, a few fowls. The vessel sailed immediately, and upon her arrival at *Bantam* the letters

---

* More commonly written *Wajū*: a race of people frequenting the rivers of Borneo and Celebes, living constantly in their boats, and said to be addicted to piracy. See Forrest's Voyage to New Guinea, Intro. p. xii, and also p. 372.

† Such the name of this gentleman appears as written in the Malayan character; but it is likely to be much corrupted.

letters and presents were duly delivered. In consequence of the advices sent, two ships were ordered to proceed without delay to *Samangka*, one of them having three and the other two masts, with three hundred soldiers on board, European and *Būgis*.* In eight days from the time of transmitting the advices, these ships made their appearance.

Kiria Minjan was in the mean time enjoying himself convivially, with the assemblage of *proatīns* at the residence of *pañgeran Wei Ratna*, and using his endeavours to prevail on them to make an attack upon the entrenchments thrown up by the Malays; when his people observing the two ships to steer for the harbour of *Samangka*, hastened to carry the intelligence to their master. " There are now," they said, " two ships " standing in towards the quarter of the Malays, and " we judge them to be sent from *Bantam* for the pro- " tection of that place." Alarmed at this information, and fearing for the consequences to himself, he instantly withdrew to his boats, set sail without loss of time, and returned to *Rātū Bagus*, near *Bantam;* making to him a report of his want of success in his mission. " Such," he said, " were the circumstances under which I left " *Samangka*. The country chiefs were unanimously " disposed to attach themselves to your cause, but the " Malays were not to be influenced by my representa-
" tions ;

* Properly the natives of a district of Celebes; but the name is commonly applied to native soldiers, in the service of Europeans, raised in any of the Eastern islands.

" tions; and the appearance of the Dutch ships rendered
" it necessary for me to return." To this recital the
Rātū uttered not a word in reply, but turned his attention
to the prosecution of the war, and from day to day
pushed on the attack against *Bantam*.

We shall now revert to the state of affairs at *Samangka*. Upon *Nakhoda Mūda's* perceiving the ships,
he summoned all the Malays to accompany him to the
landing-place, that they might be in readiness to receive
the captains; which was done with the usual compliments, as well on his own part, as that of the other
nakhodas of the place. The subject of the first inquiries
made by the captains, was, the latest accounts of the
agent of the *Rātū*; to which it was answered that he
was still supposed to be at the village of *Wei Ratna*;
but being desirous of ascertaining the fact, they dispatched the two armed praws, after putting an hundred
soldiers on board of them, with instructions to the
following effect: that if the people of the *Rātū* should
be still with the *pañgeran*, they were to send back
advice of it with all possible speed; but to remain themselves on the coast, to prevent their escape (by sea),
until they should be joined by the remainder of the force.*

Although

* To explain the seeming difficulty of praws being sent to watch an inland place, it must be understood that all the *dūsuns* or *kampongs* (which, for want of a better term, we call villages), are situated on rivers, and stationing armed vessels off the mouth of one of these, is nearly tanta- mount to investing the places on its banks. The indication of the Javanese emissaries being still in the country, would be the appearance, in or near the river, of the masted boats in which they arrived.

Although the praws left *Samangka* the same night, they could not, upon reaching the spot, see either a *panchalang* or any other vessel at the anchorage. When, on the other hand, the *pañgeran* was apprised of their arrival, he sent out people (in sampans) to look after them; and these upon their approaching the vessels, being taken on board, were asked where *Kiria Minjan* was at that time. To this they answered, that he was no longer in those parts, but had sailed for *Bantam* two nights before. A party then landed, and proceeded towards the village of the *pañgeran*, who, when he perceived them coming, gave directions for their being accommodated in one of his houses, and shortly afterwards made his appearance, but with strong marks of alarm in his countenance. Upon his asking what was the object of their visit, he was told that they were commissioned by the Dutch commanding officer to search for *Kiria Minjan*, who, they were informed, was harboured in his village. Being again assured of his having taken flight, they returned to their praws, and hastened to join their commander, to whom they communicated the intelligence.

It was now desired that *Nakhoda Mūda* should call together all the chiefs of the country, and messengers were accordingly dispatched for this purpose to every village, inviting them to repair to the Malay town. In about ten days from that time all the *pañgerans* and *proatīns*, with a proportion of their respective dependants, were collected, and such was the number of these servants

of

of God (Mahometans), that the place was not sufficient to contain them. The Dutch commander then desired of *Nakhoda Mūda*, that he would put the question to the chiefs, whether or not they were resolved to maintain their allegiance to the sultan of *Bantam* and the Company; in order that it might be clearly understood what their sentiments were. Upon this question being asked, *Wei Ratna* replied, that all the chiefs remained loyal to the sultan and the Company, as they had ever been. When the Dutch commander heard this, he said to the *pañgeran* with some warmth: " If you are really well
" affected to the government, as you now declare, what
" is the reason that you admitted into your village the
" agent of *Rātū Bagus?* Did you not know that he
" was the enemy of the sultan and the Company? If
" the news of his arrival in the country had not been
" communicated to them by *Nakhoda Mūda*, they must
" have remained ignorant of it to this hour."—" The
" cause," replied the *pañgeran*, " of my not having sent
" the intelligence was, that I had no person about me
" who was fitting to be the messenger; and besides this,
" I was under apprehension from *Kirıa*, whom I was not
" strong enough to oppose. You well know, Sir, the
" circumstances of this country; that we are not pro-
" vided with arms of a nature to defend ourselves against
" an enemy. We are all here like women in respect to
" our powers of resistance, and the sole occupation
" allowed to us by the orders of the sultan and the
" Company, is that of cultivating our plantations of
" pepper.'

" pepper." With this answer the Dutch commander appeared to be satisfied; and on a subsequent day he desired *Nakhoda Mūda* to ask whether the *proatins* would have any objection to bringing down their pepper, in order to his receiving it on account of the Company, by whose instructions he acted. This was consented to by the chiefs, and their respective dependants were directed to convey their produce to the town, from whence it was weighed off to the ships, and in three months the loading of both was completed.* They did not, however, proceed immediately to *Bantam*, but waited the event of the war with *Rātū Bagus*. When at length he was defeated, and all his adherents obliged to fly to the mountains, so that the sultan or the Company were no longer in danger of disturbance from him, the Dutch governor dispatched an order for the ships repairing to *Bantam*, which was executed without further loss of time; and upon their arrival, both the sultan and the governor were much pleased to observe the large cargoes they brought. The former directly sent a *panchālang* to *Samangka*, with a considerable number of dollars, in payment of the pepper. In this manner was business conducted by his highness and by Mynheer S.

Half a year after the return of the ships, *Nakhoda Mūda*

* The most obvious disadvantage was that experienced by the Malay traders, who were thus deprived of their freight to Java; but it is probable that the real subject of difficulty and negotiation with the chiefs, was the delivery of the pepper, in the first instance, to any other than the sultan, from whom they were accustomed to receive their payment: and for this, it is evident, the captains were not provided.

Mūda also sailed for *Bantam,* in company with all the trading praws belonging to *Samangka,* laden with cargoes of pepper. When they had proceeded as far as the narrow part of the Strait, between the land of Java and the island of *Percha* (Sumatra), the wind became foul, and *Nakhoda Mūda's* praw was wrecked on the coast between the port of *Bantam* and *Charingin.* This happened at midnight. The loading of the praw was about one hundred *bahars* (thirty tons) of pepper, of which not one grain was saved, nor any thing of value excepting the arms, which the crew carried on shore with them when they quitted the wreck; all the other vessels arrived in safety. As soon as *Nakhoda Mūda* had collected the few trifling articles that could be got at, he took with him two of his people, and proceeded to *Bantam* in a small *sampan* (canoe); where, upon his arrival, he waited on the Fiscal, and acquainted him of the accident that had befallen his praw on the coast of Java, and of the quantity of pepper that had been lost. By the Fiscal he was conducted to the governor, who, when he was informed of the event, observed, that there was no help for it, and that he, the *nakhoda,* was out of luck. After some conversation he proceeded to the house of *pañgeran Kasūma Niñgrat,* the sultan's principal and confidential minister, who had the entire administration of justice, and took cognizance of all matters, whether relating to sea or land; a minister to whom his master could with safety trust the keeping of his conscience. Having related to him his story, the

latter

latter said: " It cannot be helped: good fortune and ill
" fortune proceed from God ; and do not you, *nakhoda*,
" be the less disposed, on this account, to place your
" trust in Him. Let me know," he added, " in what
" respect I can assist you."—" My principal object,"
he replied, " in coming to make my situation known to
" your Excellency, was, to request you to accommodate
" me with the loan of a small vessel, of about two
" *koyan* burthen, for the purpose of bringing away my
" crew, with any articles they may have found the
" means of saving." A vessel properly equipped and
manned was immediately put under his orders; in
which he returned to the wreck and effected the business
intended; but upon coming back to *Bantam*, he found
his health and spirits so much impaired, that he was
obliged to confine himself to his house.

On a certain day, when the *pangeran* had an audience
of the sultan, he took an opportunity of mentioning,
that in a large fleet of praws lately arrived from *Samangka* with pepper, one vessel alone, the property of
Nakhoda Mūda, had been unfortunately wrecked on
the coast of Java; and that he (the minister) felt much
concern for the man's loss. " If *Nakhoda Mūda*," said
the sultan, " is in want of funds for carrying on his com-
" mercial dealings, supply him with whatever amount
" his occasions may require." When the *pangeran*
had taken leave and returned home, he sent for the
nakhoda. who immediately accompanied the messenger
to his presence. Upon his entering, the *pangeran* said
to

to him: " You must not suffer your mind to be dis-
" tressed. If you are in want of funds, it is the
" sultan's pleasure that you should be supplied with
" whatever sum you require, for the purchase of a
" vessel and cargo." *Nakhoda Mūda,* upon hearing
this offer, requested to be allowed a moment's time
for reflection, and then after a little consideration said:
" I beg your Excellency to be persuaded of my sincerest
" gratitude, and to accept my best acknowledgments,
" but I dare not avail myself of his highness's gracious
" intentions, by accepting of the advance, because I am
" apprehensive that in the event of my death, it might
" be the occasion of trouble to the children I shall
" leave behind me. My son is not yet experienced in
" business, nor have I myself been accustomed to employ
" a borrowed capital, but to trade on my own little
" stock, and to confine myself to the profits that it
" yielded." To this the minister replied: " If such is
" your resolution, *nakhoda,* you must not blame the
" sultan or myself for any inconvenience you may suffer.
" I am not to force upon you a royal loan that you are
" not inclined to accept."* After some further dis-
course he returned to his house at the port, where he
continued to confine himself as before; but when a
month had passed in this manner, a praw arrived from
Samangka, which his wife had dispatched to him, with
a supply of dollars to enable him to make the purchase

* The solemn exhortation of his father may probably have been the
real motive for declining this liberal offer.

of this same vessel, if he should think proper; the option being reserved to him. He bought her accordingly, complete as she stood, and having provided a cargo for her, set sail for *Samangka*, which place he reached after a navigation of only one day and one night.

It was now his design to relinquish the seafaring life, and in future to send his vessel to *Bantam*, with cargoes of pepper, consigned by letter (to a person there). He set about building a house, the dimensions of which were, ten fathoms in length and eight in depth (or breadth); the whole of the frame and boards for the sides being of teak wood. He was induced to undertake this work from the consideration that in case of his death, his son would be exempt from any trouble of that nature for twenty years to come. In about two years the building was completed; the sum expended on it not amounting to less than one thousand Spanish dollars. After this, however, he renewed his voyages to *Bantam*, and persevered in the navigation for three years. In one of his trips he made a purchase there of two praws, and took them with him to *Samangka*. To his eldest son *Wasub*, who on this occasion was distinguished by the appellation of *Nakhoda Būjang*, he gave one of these praws, fully equipped and provided, together with a trading capital. The other, with a similar outfit, he gave to his second son, named *Wasal*, who in like manner, by general assent, received the appellation of *Nakhoda Lella*. These youths had been taught all sorts of learning and accomplishments. In penmanship

penmanship especially, and the management of commercial business, their father took care to instruct them. His two sons next in age to these, named *Bantan* and *'La-uddin*, he placed under proper masters, by whom they were taught to repeat their prayers and to write.

These family concerns being arranged, he again sailed for *Bantam*, in company with several other masters of trading vessels, and attended by his two sons in their respective praws. After a short passage they arrived in safety, and, according to custom, *Nakhoda Mūda* waited upon the Fiscal and upon Governor S., to inform him of the quantity of pepper they had brought from *Samangka;* which afforded much satisfaction. In like manner he paid his compliments to the minister, to the *shabandar* (comptroller of the port), and other officers of government; after which he proceeded to deliver the pepper to the persons appointed by the sultan and the Company to receive it.

About this time the sultan having sent for his minister, and the latter, being seated in his presence, said : " Thy
" servant is come in obedience to the royal summons:
" whatever are the sultan's commands his servant is
" ready to place them on the crown of his head."—
" The occasion of my sending for you," said the sultan,
" is to express my inclination that you should bring
" hither and introduce to me *Nakhoda Mūda*, on whom
" I am disposed to confer a title, in consideration of his
" many good services to me and to the Company."—" At
" what

" what time does it please your highness that I should
" introduce him?"—" Bring him to the presence to-
" morrow morning." The minister then took leave and
returned home. As soon as morning came, he sent one
of his officers for *Nakhoda Mūda*, who instantly waited
upon him.* The *pañgeran* then made him acquainted
with the sultan's gracious intentions, and they walked
together to the fort (or castle) in which is the royal
residence. Having reached the outer, iron gate, where
the guard is stationed, they there stopped and sat down.
This guard is composed of nine officers *(pañgūlū)*, who
have each nine chosen warriors *(ūlūbalang)* under them;
and these, in succession, do duty every day; mounting
guard at the side of the iron gate. A Dutch captain
and a company of forty men also do duty there.

When the native officer and the Dutch captain
observed the approach of the *pañgeran,* accompanied
by *Nakhoda Mūda,* they asked the reason of his bringing
the latter. " It is," said he, " in consequence of orders
" from the sultan himself, that I am going to introduce
" him to the presence." The officers were all very much
astonished at hearing this, and said among themselves:
" What can be the intention of the sultan in sending
" for this man? How many *nakhodas* of great wealth
" and influence have visited *Bantam,* from various parts
" of

* The translator has judged it proper to abridge these messages and
replies, which in the original are given with tedious repetition; but the
ceremonies of introduction that follow, although ridiculously circum-
stantial, being characteristic of manners, he thinks it necessary to
preserve.

"of Java, and yet not one of them, that ever we have "known or heard of, has been sent for by the sultan in "this manner, to enter his castle." Such were the reflections made by the guard, both natives and Europeans.* The *pañgeran* then said to one of the persons on duty: "Go you to *Fakir Adam*,† and acquaint "him that I am attending here, on the outside of the "iron gate, accompanied by *Nakhoda Mūda*, in order "to his being introduced to the presence." One of the guard thereupon went to find *Fakir Adam*, and informed him that the *pañgeran* and *Nakhoda Mūda* were in waiting to be admitted. "Request his Excellency," said the *Fakir*, "to come hither to my apartment." The guard, on his return, acquainted the *pañgeran* that *Fakir Adam* requested him to come to his apartment; which he and the *nakhoda* did accordingly. In this apartment or saloon, where the *Fakir* was stationed, there was an assemblage of about forty persons, some of whom were skilled in performances (or exercises) after the manner of the Arabs,‡ and in playing on all kinds

of

* This seems to be a little indulgence of personal vanity, on the part of the auto-biographer.

† He appears to have held an office in the sultan's household corresponding to that of our master of the ceremonies, or of the revels. His name is singularly contrasted with his duties; but from its sanctified import, it is probable that he may have had the superintendence of the *haram*.

‡ The text says, "skilled in playing with, or performing the *dabūs*," after the Arabian manner. In the dictionaries we find the word دبوس translated by 'club or mace;' but such weapons seem ill calculated for amusement in the interior of a palace.

of musical instruments, and others in dancing according to the Javanese mode. These exhibitions, of which *Fakir Adam* had the direction, were provided for the amusement of the sultan, who came to the saloon whenever he was inclined to enjoy any particular sport. Upon the *pañgeran's* making his appearance, *Fakir Adam* inquired his reason for bringing the *nakhoda* with him. " I know not," he replied, " any thing more " of the circumstances leading to this introduction, than " that the sultan expressed to me his pleasure that I " should this day conduct him to the presence." *Fakir Adam* appeared to be much surprised, and could not form any conjecture respecting the sultan's further intentions. " Go," said the *pañgeran*, " and intimate to his high- " ness that I am in your apartment, together with " *Nakhoda Mūda*, waiting to be admitted to the pre- " sence." *Fakir Adam* then proceeded to convey the information to the sultan, as desired. Upon reaching the apartment where the female attendants are stationed,* an elderly woman who had the superintendence of the others, as soon as she perceived him, said: " What is " *Fakir Adam's* object in coming hither?"—" My good " mother," he replied, " my business is to give infor- " mation that *pañgeran Kasūma Niñgrat*, together " with *Nakhoda Mūda*, are desirous of paying their
" respects

* In many courts of the further East the interior guard of the palace is composed of females, who in some instances (as at Achin) are regularly trained to arms. They are probably thought to be less dangerous to their masters than embodied slaves of the other sex, by whom dynasties have been so often overturned.

" respects to his highness, and that these personages
" are now in my apartment awaiting his commands."
Having heard this message, the old female withdrew,
and upon repairing to the presence was asked by the
sultan the occasion of her coming. " My reason," said
she, " for approaching the throne is to report that
" pañgeran Kasūma Niñgrat, together with Nakhoda
" Mūda, are now in the apartment of Fakir Adam,
" waiting for permission to pay their respects to your
" majesty."—" Order them," said the sultan, " to ap-
" proach." The old female bowed and retired, in order
to make known to Fakir Adam the sultan's orders for
their admission; upon which the fakir returned to them,
and signified the sultan's pleasure that they should be
admitted to the presence-chamber.* Upon receiving
this intimation they immediately proceeded thither, and
having made the customary obeisance, sat down in the
presence.† The sultan then, addressing himself to the
pañgeran, said : " It is my pleasure this day to confer on
" Nakhoda Mūda the title of Kei Damáng Perwasídana.
" Be it your care to notify it to the nine officers of the
" guard and to the Dutch captain, who do duty at the
" outer gate of my fort, as well as to my subjects gene-
" rally, in the city of Bantam." Upon hearing these
(gracious)

---

* It is not to be presumed that such formal delays attended the
minister's usual visits; but it was consistent with the sultan's dignity that
every ceremonial and etiquette should be observed on this occasion.

† Sitting down in the presence of a superior is, in the East, a respectful
posture, as standing is in Europe.

(gracious) words from the sultan, *Nakhoda Mūda* made his obeisance to the illustrious throne, and then said: " Pardon, my liege, your servant, who avows his
" wish that he might not be distinguished by any other
" appellation than that which he has hitherto, and for a
" long time borne; but who is at the same time aware
" that it is his duty to bow his head to the commands of
" his sovereign; and since the royal word cannot be
" revoked, in consequence of any thing that he can urge,
" the will of his master must be done."* When he had thus spoken, he asked permission to retire; but the sultan ordered the female attendants to present to him a change of dress, consisting of a cap, a robe, and drawers of scarlet cloth, together with a sabre, a lance, a kris, and a large umbrella. As soon as the investiture of these was completed, they paid their compliments and departed; the *pañgeran* taking care to anounce to the officers on guard at the outer gate, the new title conferred on the *nakhoda*, and desiring to have it properly signified to the inhabitants of the city; which they cheerfully promised to execute. After some conversation together, the *pañgeran* returned to his house, and *Kei Damáng* to his vessel.

On the following morning he paid his respects to the Dutch governor, and after wishing him health, gave an account of the sultan's having commanded his attendance, and

* There is some degree of obscurity in the latter part of this courtly acquiescence, perhaps from the omission of a word; but the general sense is given in the translation.

and of his highness being graciously pleased to bestow on him a title similar to those borne by the nobles of the land of Java; as also of his having requested to be allowed the indulgence of retaining his original appellation, but in which he could not prevail. The governor was pleased to say, that if the sultan had not anticipated him by conferring a title, it was his intention to have done it on the part of the Dutch Company; but that his purpose was now equally answered. He then produced a double-barrel gun and a pair of double-barrel pistols. " How much, Sir," says *Kei Damáng*, " may " be the price of these arms?"—" It is not my design," replied the governor, " to sell them, but to present them " to you as a gift." *Kei Damáng* made his acknowledgments, took leave, and returned to his vessel. Alongside of her he found two men, in a small boat, who had brought a barrel of gunpowder and a cask of bullets, which, upon his inquiring from whence and on what account they were sent, he learned to be a gift from the captain of the guard. He gave directions for stowing them away in the praw, and desired the men to carry back to the captain his grateful thanks.

He then called together all the masters who had accompanied him from *Samangka*, and communicated to them the information of the sultan and the Company having been pleased to confer a title on him. " It was " not," he added, " of my seeking, nor did it accord with " my wishes. The honour may perhaps be attended with " good, or, perhaps with bad consequences to me." The

nakhodas

nakhodas hereupon gave their several opinions, some arguing favourably, and some unfavourably to the measure. " Be it as it may," continued *Kei Damáng*, " there is no help for it. The sultan and the Company " have laid the burthen on me. The matter cannot be " undone. Placed as I am, under their government, it " is not my inclination, but their will, that must take " effect. I commit myself to the care of the Almighty, " from whom both prosperity and adversity proceed." The *nakhodas* then repaired to their respective vessels, in order to equip them for sea, and to prepare cargoes of merchandize for their returning voyage. *Kei Damáng* waited on the *pañgeran* to take leave, and then paid the same compliment to the governor, acquainting him that he, together with all the Malay traders, were making ready to sail. " 'Tis well," said the governor. " Let " it be your care, *Kei Damáng*, to prevent the chiefs of " the *Lampōng* villages from quarrelling amongst them- " selves; and when their pepper is sufficiently dried, do " not suffer them to keep it unnecessarily long in the " country." Soon after this conversation the fleet of praws sailed, and effected the passage in a short time. Thus did the traders of *Samangka* employ themselves annually.

About three years from the period of these transactions had elapsed, when two soldiers (of the country-guard) arrived from *Croee* (an English settlement in the south-western part of Sumatra), with a letter to *Kei Damáng* from Mr. Norris, the chief of that place, the

purport

MALAYAN FAMILY. 41

purport of which was to request that he would forward these messengers, with their dispatches, to Batavia, where Mr. Garden, an Englishman, was at that time agent for all the gentlemen belonging to the establishment of Bencoolen.* They were accordingly furnished with a conveyance to Batavia. In that same month accounts were received of Bencoolen being attacked by the French; † in consequence of which many of the inhabitants of *Croee* removed (for safety) to *Samangka*, and presented themselves to *Kei Damáng*, who said to them: " Dwell here, my brethren, along with me. Do " not feel any apprehension about the French, nor " uneasiness on account of this place being within the " jurisdiction of the Dutch Company, for as soon as " tranquillity shall be restored at Bencoolen, if it be " then your inclination to return to *Croee*, you may " freely do it." Five months after the departure of the French from Bencoolen, according to the intelligence received, a praw sent from *Bantam* by the sultan and the

* The object of this dispatch by the way of Batavia, was probably to order an insurance to be effected in England on property at Fort Marlborough; which eventually gave occasion to a celebrated trial in the Court of King's Bench, before Lord Mansfield; payment, after the capture, being resisted, on the ground of the indemnity afforded by the insurance having weakened the exertions to defend the place; for which there was but too much colour. The decision, however, went against the Underwriters. Vid. Carter and Boehm, 3d Burrow, 1905, and 1st Blackstone, 593.

† Bencoolen (Fort Marlborough) was captured by a French squadron, under the Comte d'Estaing, in the month of April, 1760, and evacuated in the course of the year. A clue is thus afforded to all the dates of preceding and subsequent events.

the governor, touched at *Samangka*, with orders to *Kei Damáng* to put on board at this place, a person well acquainted with *Croee;* which being done accordingly, she sailed for that settlement, and having taken in the pepper found there, returned with it to *Bantam.* Shortly after this transaction the news of the re-establishment of the English Company at Bencoolen became known, and the sultan sent no more vessels to *Croee* for pepper.*

About a year after these proceedings it happened that two *nakhodas* of *Samangka*, one of them named *Nakhoda Satia*, and the other *Nakhoda Dūgam*, made a trip to *Bantam* with pepper, and having delivered their cargoes, purchased merchandize suited to the market of Bencoolen; with which they returned (in the first instance) to *Samangka*. Here they repaired their praws, gave them new masts, and then reshipped the goods they had brought. *Kei Damáng* (observing this) asked them to what place they were bound. They replied, to Bencoolen. " You must not," said he, " proceed to " Bencoolen: it is contrary to the orders of the Dutch " Company; and if you persist, you will certainly bring " mischief upon yourselves."—" Do not," they answered, " be under alarm for any mischief that may happen
" to

---

* It is probable that this pepper (which must have been English, not native property, because it was always paid for when warehoused) became the plunder of individuals, and was not carried to the account of the Dutch Company. An inveterate spirit of hostility and aggression, however, subsisted between the servants of these rival Companies, although the nations were at peace.

" to us; we have both of us wit enough for our own
" security."—" No matter for your wit," replied *Kei
Damáng;* " be what it may, you are not to go to Ben-
" coolen." The two *nakhodas* made no answer to this,
but were not diverted from their purpose, and when
night came they set sail.

In the following year a *panchálang* arrived from *Bantam,* the master of which, named *Nakhoda Jāmīl,* had
orders to apply to *Kei Damáng* for the assistance of
thirty men, along with whom he was to proceed
to *Croee,* for the purpose of seeing the state of that
place.* " What end," said *Kei Damáng,* " will your
" going to *Croee* answer, since we have intelligence of
" the English being re-established at Bencoolen?"—" It
" is no matter," replied *Jāmīl:* " the governor's positive
" orders are that I should march thither."† He was
accordingly furnished with the thirty men, and after a
month had been employed on the expedition, he returned
to *Samangka,* in consequence of his learning that the
governor of Bencoolen had dispatched on official person
to the place, whom he *(Jāmīl)* had no desire to meet.
Previously to his leaving *Samangka,* for *Bantam,* he
chanced to fall in with *Nakhoda Satia* and *Nakhoda
Dugām,* who had returned from Bencoolen. Upon his
arrival at *Bantam* he found that Mynheer Sambirik (?)
was

---

* The apparent intention of this expedition was to take possession of
the English settlement, if found unoccupied.

† The distance across the country, from *Samangka* to *Croee,* on the
western coast, is not considerable.

was no longer the governor, having been removed to *Samārang*, with the rank of Edele Heer (one of the council), and that his successor at *Bantam* was Mynheer Poer. To the latter, therefore, he made his report: that he was just arrived from Croee, whither he had been sent by the former governor, to inspect the state of the place; but that at the time of his arrival there, an officer deputed by the governor of Bencoolen, came to take charge of the settlement. " It cannot be helped," said the new governor: " If those to whom the country " belongs return to it, we can no longer have any wish " respecting it." After some further conversation, he departed, and called at the house of Ensign *Si-Tālib*, a half-caste native of *Macassar*, who was made an officer at *Bantam*.* This person inquired of *Jāmil* what news he brought from *Samangka*. " I bring nothing new," he replied, " excepting that I saw two *nakhodas* who " were just arrived from Bencoolen, about the time of " my departure." The ensign asked him whether he had given information of this circumstance to the governor. He said he had not yet mentioned it to any one but himself. On the next morning they went together to wait on Mynheer Poer, when *Si-Tālib* informed him that in a certain country called *Samangka*, which lay within his jurisdiction, it was the constant practice to slip out praws every season, for the voyage to Bencoolen. " Whilst this man *Jāmil*," added he,
" was

---

* He may probably have commanded the country-guard, which gave him consequence amongst the natives.

" was on the spot, there were two praws just returned
" from that place, which had been dispatched by the
" head-man of *Samangka*, whose title is *Kei Damáng*
" *Perwasīdana*; a title given to him by the sultan and
" the late governor, Mynheer S., as a reward for his care
" of the district, and particularly for keeping a watchful
" eye upon any intercourse by praws with Bencoolen.
" He is now become a person of considerable conse-
" quence and wealth, insomuch that no one there can
" cope with him."—" Does he ever," said the governor,
" come to *Bantam?* If he comes, I shall lay a fine
" upon him."—" I left him," answered *Jāmīl*, " building
" a praw, with the intention of loading her with pepper
" for this place." Having told this story, they both
retired. The reason of the ensign's malevolence was the
neglect with which he had found himself treated by all
the people who came from *Samangka* during the government of Mynheer S., from whom he met with no
countenance; whereas, after the arrival of Mynheer
Poer, he was in particular favour, was treated as a
confidential person, and consulted upon every occasion.
In short, the governor's kindness to him was unbounded.

About five months had elapsed when *Kei Damáng*
arrived at *Bantam*, with a fleet of twelve praws, all
fully laden with pepper; among which number were
those commanded by his sons, *Nakhoda Būjang* and
Nakhoda Lella. His younger sons, *Si-Bantan* and
'*La-uddīn*, likewise accompanied him. The Fiscal, to
whom

whom he paid the customary visit and reported the number and cargoes of the vessels, recommended the masters' going together to wait on the governor, who, he informed them, was a different person from him under whose orders they formerly acted: of which change *Kei Damáng* professed himself ignorant. Being arrived at the castle where the governor resided, and the usual[1] salutations upon entrance being made, the Fiscal said: " This is the person who bears the title of *Kei Damáng* " *Perwasidana*; whose business it is to superintend the " country of *Lampóng-Samangka*, under the orders of " the Company and the sultan, and to take cognizance " of all disputes amongst the inhabitants."—" I am " come," added *Kei Damáng*, " with a fleet of twelve " praws all fully laden with pepper: but it is incumbent " on me to mention to your honour a circumstance that " has occurred, of two praws having sailed to Bencoolen " without my knowledge; which have since returned, " and are now at *Samangka*."—" Do not suppose," replied the governor, " that you are the first to give me " information of this proceeding. I am already well " acquainted with it." They then took their leave, and *Kei Damáng* waited on the *pañgeran* (sultan's minister), who expressed much satisfaction to hear of the arrival of so many cargoes of pepper.*

After an interval of about a month from that time, the governor ordered *Kei Damáng* to appear before him; and

---

* In the profit on which he probably participated with his master.

and he promptly obeyed the summons. As soon as his entrance was observed, the governor said to him : " The " occasion on which I have sent for you is the affair " of the two praws that went to Bencoolen. Of the " parties themselves I know nothing, but must look to " you as the responsible person. Your's rather than " their's is the blame, inasmuch as it was your duty to " have prevented them; and I have no doubt in my " own mind but that you yourself dispatched them to " that place. On these charges I condemn you, *Kei* " *Damáng*, to pay a fine of two hundred Spanish " dollars." Upon hearing this speech from the governor he said, " Sir, I positively deny the charge of having " been in any way concerned in the dispatch of those " vessels. If the contrary can be proved against me, " I am ready to submit to any penalty that you may " think proper to inflict."—" My sentence," said the governor, " must not be disputed. Let the two hun- " dred dollars be brought to me to-morrow morning."* *Kei Damáng*, upon this, returned to his praw, and sent to call together the *nakhodas* who had accompanied him from *Samangka*. When assembled, he stated to them the circumstance of his being summoned before the governor on account of the two praws having made a voyage to Bencoolen, and accused of having a concern in their dispatch; of his being brought to disgrace, and condemned

---

* There is much reason to suspect that this fine went into the pocket of the judge.

condemned to pay a penalty of two hundred dollars. "What advice," he asked, " do you, my friends, give " me on the subject of this business?"—" In our " opinion," replied the *nakhodas,* " your most eligible " proceeding will be to represent your hardship to the " sultan's minister; for all of us know well (and can bear " testimony to him), that you neither ordered nor per- " mitted *Nakhoda Sātia* and *Nakhoda Dūgam* to go to " Bencoolen. If the governor should then still persist " in levying a penalty, we have spirit enough, what- " ever it may be, to raise it among us."—" It does not " appear to me," said *Kei Damáng,* " that such appeal " to the *pañgeran* can produce any good effect, but " will rather have the appearance of opposition to the " authority of the Company. It will be better that I " pay the fine at once. My chief object in stating the " matter to you, was to shew you the injustice and " oppression I experience from persons in power; for in " my own conscience I am free from all offence, either " to the Company, the sultan, or the chiefs of the " *Samangka* country. But there is no help for it, and " I resign myself to the protection of God. The con- " duct of the two *nakhodas* has brought me into this " trouble; but even if my life be made answerable for " the acts of those with whom I am connected, I can " only recommend myself to the Almighty (and bow to " his decree)."—" If," said the *nakhodas,* " you think " it best to submit to the fine (without further remon- " strance), we will assist you to make up the sum of

" two

"two hundred dollars." They accordingly furnished one hundred and fifty dollars among them, and *Kei Damáng* paid the remaining fifty. Such was the conduct on this occasion of the traders who came together from *Samangka*.

The fine having been paid, the governor ordered *Kei Damáng* to return to *Samangka* with the fleet of praws, on board of which he put four Dutch soldiers, with a corporal, whose name was Raūs,* and his wife. The reason assigned by Mynheer Poer, to the sultan, for this measure was, that they might serve as a guard to the Dutch colours: "for," said he, "if the Company have "not some establishment of its own at *Samangka*, the "place will certainly be taken possession of by the "English." *Kei Damáng* accordingly sailed with these five men and one woman, for whom, upon his arrival, he built a house; towards the expense of which the Company did not contribute one *copper cash*. It was all defrayed by *Kei Damáng* and the other Malays of the place, who lent their assistance to erect the building and to make a proper fence round it. Besides this burthen they were obliged to put up with very harsh language from the corporal, whenever there was any delay in performing what he ordered to be done. Nay, he even went so far as to strike them. Four different Malays were struck by him, because they were not sufficiently expeditious in completing his hen-house. Three months after

---

* Perhaps Roos or Rouse.

after this, eight more Dutch soldiers arrived, one of whom was a serjeant, together with his wife; making in all, thirteen men and two women, in the country of *Lampŏng-Samangka.*

Eighteen months subsequently to the coming of these soldiers, an English two-masted vessel, from Bencoolen, made her appearance (in the bay). As soon as she was perceived by the serjeant, he called to *Kei Damáng* and acquainted him of the approach of an English ship. " Her colours," said he, " I can distinguish with my " spying-glass."—" And may I ask," said *Kei Damáng,* " what are the governor's instructions to you, in case of " the arrival of any ship, whether Dutch or English?"— " His instructions," answered the serjeant, " are to " hoist our colours: further than this I have none."— " The orders," said *Kei Damáng,* " that I received from " the former governor were, when a ship, from what- " ever country, should appear, to send out a boat to " pilot her to the proper anchorage; and if she should " fire a salute, to return it from the shore." The serjeant and the corporal approved of this, and proposed that one of them, together with *Nakhoda Bŭjang,* should go off in a boat to visit the ship. Corporal Raūs and the *nakhoda* accordingly went off in a *sampan* (canoe) with four paddles. When they reached the vessel, the captain, whose name was Forrest,* asked

Raūs,

* This was the Captain Thomas Forrest, afterwards so well known in the history of oriental navigation, by his ' Voyage to New Guinea' in the year 1774, performed in a vessel of ten tons burthen; and by other

Raūs, which was the best spot for anchoring. "I "cannot inform you," said he, "you must inquire of "the *nakhoda*, who is acquainted with the harbour." The latter having pointed it out, the ship was brought to an anchor there; after which the captain went on shore along with them, and proceeded to the Dutch quarters. As soon as this was known to *Kei Damáng*, he waited upon him there, and paid the usual compliments of civility; which the captain returned, inquiring at the same time of the corporal, who the person that addressed him was. *Raūs* informed him that he was the chief man of the place, appointed by the governor and the sultan to manage all their affairs at *Samangka*. After this had passed Captain Forrest returned to his ship, but at eight o'clock the next morning relanded, and proceeded as before to the quarters of Corporal Raūs. He now desired that he might be supplied with fowls, ducks, goats, and other articles of which he stood in need.

nautical publications. He was a man of enterprize in his prófession, and a ready draughtsman, but not always quite careful enough to distinguish (as Alexander Dalrymple the great hydrographer used to observe) between what he actually saw and what he imagined to exist. His manners were eccentric in a high degree, and many entertaining stories of his adventures amongst the natives were current in India; such, for instance, as the following: Having advanced some way from the shore, in an island where he touched, and finding the people disposed to be troublesome or hostile, he quietly took out his german flute, and having adjusted it, began to play an air of Correlli, which surprised, amused, and caused them to suspend their designs, whilst he, keeping his face towards them, gradually retreated to the place where he had left his boat's crew. To this singular person the translator is indebted for his first introduction to Sir Joseph (then Mr.) Banks, in January of the year 1780.

need. The Dutchman begged he would not take it amiss, when he declared himself incapable of furnishing what he required, acquainting him that he had not been long at the place, and that he was himself under the necessity of applying for what he wanted to *Kei Damáng*, who possessed the whole influence. His business, he said, was merely to guard the Company's colours, under the orders of Mynheer Poer, the governor of *Bantam*. The captain, upon this information, sent a message, in his own name and that of the serjeant, to *Kei Damáng*, requesting him to come to the guard-house. He came accordingly, and after the usual compliments paid and returned, Corporal Raüs said to him:* " Our " reason for wishing to see you is, that the captain has " made application to be supplied with live stock."— " And what," replied *Kei Damáng*, " do you, the " corporal and serjeant, say to this application?"—" It " is not," they answered, " any concern of ours; but " if you can be of any service to the captain, assist " him as far as you have the means."—" You will do " me a favour," said the captain, " by procuring me " stock for my sea store." In consequence of what was said to him by the Dutchmen, as well as by the English captain, *Kei Damáng* replied: " It is well, Captain; I " shall endeavour to assist you with what you require, " but

* There is some confusion in the narrative between the persons and rank of the serjeant and corporal; but the latter may probably have been the more intelligent of the two, or more versed in the language of the country, which occasioned him to be the spokesman.

" but you must allow me till to-morrow morning to
" execute it. If I can prove useful to you, do not
" consider it as a favour, and if I fail, do not be dis-
" pleased with me." After this conversation Captain
Forrest again returned to his ship, and *Kei Damáng*
asked the serjeant his deliberate opinion as to the pro-
priety of his supplying the fresh provisions. " It
" cannot," said he, " be of any consequence: supply
" them if you can." Upon returning home he gave
directions to his people to go (into the country) and
collect poultry, which was done, and by the time the
captain came on shore in the morning, he found a sufficient provision of all that he wanted. Captain Forrest's
stay at *Samangka* was ten days in the whole, and he
then took his departure; but the course of his navigation was not certainly known.

Four days after the sailing of this vessel, Ensign
Si-Talib arrived from *Bantam*. He was bound to Bencoolen, but prevented from reaching it by a contrary
wind.* Calling upon *Kei Damáng*, he said: " I was
" dispatched to Bencoolen by Governor Poer, with a
" cargo of rice. My instructions were, in case I could
" not get so far as that place, to stop at *Croee*, and
" dispose of my cargo there, or, if I could not reach
" *Croee*, to put into *Samangka*. I shall now deliver
" the rice into your hands, for my orders were, on no
" account to carry it back to *Bantam*." Upon receiving
this

* From whence it may be inferred that this was about the setting in of
the north-west monsoon, in the month of November.

this notice, *Kei Damáng* called a meeting of all the *nakhodas* of *Samangka*, to whom he stated the circumstances that had just been communicated to him, and asked their opinion as to what was to be done with the rice. They were at a loss what to advise; for the cargo, which amounted to ten *koyan* (or eight thousand gallons), was Java rice, and much damaged by weevils.* *Si-Talīb* urged them to a determination. " What I " should recommend," said a man named *Nakhoda Semporna*, " would be, in the first instance, to dispose of a " part at the different rivers in *Samangka* bay, and by " that means ascertain the price that the remainder " ought to fetch."—" As to the price," said the ensign, interrupting him, " the governor has fixed that at " twelve bamboos (gallons) the Spanish dollar."—" But " if it will not go off at that rate," said *Semporna,* " what is to be done?" Here the conversation ended, and *Kei Damáng* directed one of his sons, *Nakhoda Lella*, to load a boat with two *koyan* of the rice, and endeavour to dispose of it; which occupied him two months. In the course of three months, however, that the ensign remained at *Samangka*, the whole was sold.

During this period *Si-Talīb* concerted a plot with Raūs, the serjeant of the Dutch guard,† for the ruin of

* The rice exported from Java and Balli is generally of inferior quality, imperfectly cleared of the inner husk, and has the grains much broken. It is consequently not in demand, unless in times of scarcity, among people who cultivate the article for themselves.

† Here the confusion of persons is palpable, excepting on the supposition that Raūs had been promoted, and appointed to the command of the guard.

of *Kei Damáng*. " I should like," said the ensign to the serjeant, " to reside at this place."—" But what " object," replied the other, " could it be to you to " reside here, seeing that all the power is in the hands " of *Kei Damáng*? How could you expect to have an " influence superior to that of a man who has been so " long connected in the country?"—" If you will enter " into my views," said *Si-Talīb*, " we could contrive " a plan—that is, if you are well inclined."—" What- " ever you have to say," replied the serjeant, " speak " out, that I may understand you." Upon which the ensign proceeded thus: " Do you, serjeant, write a " letter, and send it to the governor of *Bantam*. In " this letter, state that *Kei Damáng* sold pepper to the " English ship that touched here lately, and never paid " regard to any remonstrances that you made to him on " the subject. Make use of my name, and say that I " am well acquainted with his proceedings. Do not dis- " patch the letter till I am gone; but in such time that " it shall arrive at *Bantam* soon after me; when the " governor will naturally make inquiry of me respecting " the truth of the charges. If we can succeed in getting " *Kei Damáng* removed from *Samangka*, and you and " I should have the future management of the country, " we could certainly make it turn to good account." The serjeant having listened to all this, and approved of the scheme, recommended that the other should lose no time in returning to *Bantam*. " I hear," said he, " there is a praw nearly ready to sail for that place,
" with

"with pepper, and by this conveyance I can send the "letter, which I shall give in charge to my wife." This matter being arranged, *Si-Talib* set out, and ten days after his departure, *Nakhoda Inchi Lāūt*, in whose vessel serjeant Raūs sent his wife, with the letter for the governor, sailed also. Thirteen days after *Si-Talib's* arrival, the letter followed, and was delivered by the woman to Mynheer Poer: who read the contents, which were such has had been concerted. It concluded by desiring, that if the writer was not to be credited on his word, inquiry should be made of *Si-Talib*, who was at *Samangka* about the time it happened. When the governor had perused it, he sent for the ensign and asked him what news there was when he visited the place. "The news I heard," said *Si-Talib*, " was, " that an English ship from Bencoolen, commanded by " a Captain Forrest, had touched there. That *Kei* " *Damáng* had sold pepper to this captain, and was " subservient to his will in every circumstance; not " paying regard to any advice given to him by the " serjeant."—" And what is the reason," said the governor, " that I have been kept so long in ignorance " of this transaction?"—" The reason of my silence on " the subject," replied *Si-Talib*, " was my fear that I " should be considered in the light of a calumniator." The governor said nothing further, and the ensign returned to his own house.

Nakhoda Inchi Lāūt, together with the masters of the other praws of the season, sailed on their returning voyage,

voyage, and on board of his vessel the governor sent back the serjeant's wife, and at the same time three Dutch soldiers. About a month after their arrival at *Samangka*, a two-masted vessel called a ketch, made her appearance. As soon as she was perceived by *Kei Damáng*, he went to the serjeant and asked him what sort of vessel he supposed that to be; observing that it looked something like a ship.* The serjeant said he knew nothing about her: it might be a ship or it might not. " What are the orders," said the former, " in " case she should anchor here and fire a salute? Am I " to return the salute, or not?"—" Do not return it; " as if we affected to make ourselves of equal conse- " quence with these people (European captains). Who " knows where she may come from? We know nothing " about her." As she approached, the Dutch colours were distinguished, and the serjeant called *Nakhoda Būjang* to accompany him to the vessel. When they reached her, they paid their compliments to the captain. Upon the ketch's coming to an anchor, a salute was fired by her gunner, and the captain went on shore. *Kei Damáng* waited his landing at the mouth of the river. When they met, the captain addressed him in an angry tone, saying: " What is the reason that you did " not return my salute? Do you imagine yourself a " person

---

* A ketch has a main-mast and a small mizen-mast, as a brig has a main and fore-mast. The Malay word *kapal*, which we translate ship, is not confined to one with three masts, but applied to any square-rigged vessel, with top and top-gallant masts.

" person of more consequence than me, that you do not
" condescend to return my civility?"—" The reason,"
answered *Kei Damáng*, " that your salute was not
" answered was, my being guided by the advice of
" serjeant Raus, who gave it as his opinion that in case
" of a salute being fired from the ship, it ought not to
" be returned." The captain was still dissatisfied, and
asked why any weight should be allowed to what the
serjeant advised? *Kei Damáng* did not make any
reply, judging that it would answer no good purpose
to get into an altercation. They separated, and the
captain went back to his vessel.

On the following morning he landed again, and gave
directions for calling together all the inhabitants of the
Malay town; on which occasion he took down their
names in writing; and this being done, he said to *Kei
Damáng:* " Order all these people to set about con-
" structing a stockade."* He himself measured out
the ground and formed the plan; the dimensions being
forty fathoms on every side. *Kei Damáng* inquired
whether for the erection of the fort, those persons only
who inhabited the Malay town were to be put in re-
quisition, or whether the country (native) chiefs were
to be called upon to lend their assistance; as, in the
former case, he thought it would be a long time before
the work could be completed. The captain desired him
to suggest that mode which he thought would tend to
its

* This measure of fortifying the place we may presume to have been
the consequence of Captain Forrest's visit.

its more effectual execution, and he would take it into consideration. " In my opinion," said *Kei Damáng*, " the *proatins* should be required to contribute their " share (of the labour and materials). In this country of " *Lampōng-Sāmangka* there is a chief called *pañgeran* " *Wei Ratna*, who is the first person in rank and con- " sequence, and to him the captain will do well to make " application." They accordingly proceeded together to the village where this chief resided, when the captain addressed him in the following words: " I am come to " wait on the *pañgeran*," said he, " in pursuance of " directions from the governor of *Bantam*, to examine " into the state of this district, which it is his intention " to put on a footing similar to that of the sea-coast of " Java. In the part (of the bay) occupied by the " Malays I observe a situation proper for the erection " of a fort, and the *pañgeran* and *Kei Damáng* must " employ a sufficient number of people to execute " the work in a satisfactory manner."—" It is well, " captain," replied the *pañgeran*; " but you must " allow me a little time for preparation. In five days " I shall be ready to go down, and pay attention to the " business." The captain returned with *Kei Damáng* to the Malay town, and on the next day he proposed that they should go together to examine the boundary mark that separated the territory of the English from that of the Dutch Company; at a place that bore the name of *Muara Tanda* (demarcation-river-mouth). They accordingly proceeded thither; the captain being in one

sailing-

sailing-boat, and *Kei Damáng*, with two of his sons, *Nakhoda Bújang* and *Si-Bantan*, in a second; the other sons, *Nakhoda Lella* and *'La-uddin*, remaining behind to take care of the house. Upon their arrival at the spot, the captain gave orders for removing the mark, and took away with him the English notice of the limits (inscription?)* After passing three nights there, they returned towards *Samangka*, the captain taking a seat in *Kei Damáng's* boat. When they drew near to the ketch, the former said: " Let us step on board of my vessel " before we go any further, and amuse ourselves for an " hour or two."—" With much pleasure," answered *Kei Damáng*, " I shall be gratified to see how things " are arranged in your ships." *Kei Damáng* thereupon went on board.

At this moment serjeant Raūs (who observed what was passing afloat) called on *Nakhoda Lella* and *'La-uddin*, and said to them : " Come along ; let us also go " on board of the ketch, and bring your father and the " captain, as well as your younger brothers, on shore." They did not hesitate to accompany him, and went off in a sampan, which was rowed by those three persons. Upon *Nakhoda Lella's* stepping into the vessel, the serjeant and the captain required him to lay aside his kris (loosen his kris-belt); to which he answered that

his

---

* This was probably a plate of metal, and perhaps inlaid in a block of stone; which may account for its being spoken of as something distinct from the land-mark itself, which must have been common to both nations. The terms by which the former is expressed in the original are *tunjuk tanāh*, ' what points out the land.'

his continuing to wear it could be a matter of no consequence; for even in the fort of *Bantam* it was not refused to him. As soon as *Kei Damáng* heard their voices in this altercation, he desired his son to make no words about it, but to do as the captain desired him, and to give up his kris. Upon receiving his father's orders he loosed it from his girdle and gave it to one of the people; *'La-uddīn* doing the same. They then went into the cabin, and sat down near their father and their two brothers. When they were all thus seated together, the captain addressed *Kei Damáng* in these words: " You and your four sons are no longer at " liberty to quit this vessel. I have the governor's " orders for carrying you away from hence, and for this " purpose it was that I came to *Samangka*."—" It is " well, Sir," replied he; " but you took unnecessary " trouble in coming here for the purpose; because a " mere slip of paper transmitted to me, would have met " with implicit obedience from one who has ever con- " sidered himself as living under the control of the " Company." After this the captain went on shore and proceeded to the house of *Kei Damáng*, which he ordered the military under arms to surround, whilst he and the serjeant entered it. All the property was seized upon, and four days were employed in transporting it to the ketch; the captain and his people remaining in possession of the house day and night. Every day a buffaloe was killed for their provision, and they passed their time in eating, drinking, and making merry.

In

In the mean time *Kei Damáng* and his four sons were guarded on board by a Dutch corporal and a party of men. Their food, both meat and drink, was supplied to them from the houses of his brothers, named *Nakhoda Darman* and *Nakhoda Semporna*, who themselves came off every day, bringing with them such articles as their occasions might require; but whatever they brought on board was first shewn to the guard for examination, and afterwards delivered to the prisoners. This was the regular practice. On a certain day *Nakhoda Semporna* visited the captain (on shore), carrying a present (according to the eastern usage) of some of the nests of the bird called *láyang-láyang* (edible bird's nest), and said to him: " I am come, captain, to inquire of you " your opinion whether *Kei Damáng* and his four sons " will be permitted to return to *Samangka*, or not."— " What," said he, " is your motive for asking the " question?"—" It is this: I am myself not properly " an inhabitant of *Samangka*, but of the Malay quarter " at Batavia, and am here only on *Kei Damáng's* " account, in consequence of his having shewn me kind- " ness.* If he is not to return to this place, I shall go " back to Batavia."—" I know not how that matter " may be," replied the captain. " Possibly he may not " be allowed to return; for it is reported that his " offences against the Company are of a serious nature.

" I

* The trouble experienced by *Kei Damáng* in the affair of the two praws that went to Bencooolen, and his being fined in consequence, must have been the occasion of this friendly visit from his brothers.

"I have heard it mentioned that he has been guilty of "selling pepper to the English."* *Nakhoda Semporna* said nothing further, but took his leave, and, as he was accustomed to do, carried victuals on board; which afforded him an opportunity of communicating to *Kei Damáng* the reason assigned by the captain for his detension. "Do not," he replied, "feel any uneasiness "for me on that score. I have committed no offence "either against the Company or the sultan, and I trust "to the protection of the Almighty. If I am to be "ruined (in this world), I shall still be found innocent "in the sight of God."

After *Nakhoda Semporna's* return on shore, *Nakhoda Būjang* and *Nakhoda Lella* thus addressed their father: "Do not, our respected father, consume more time in "(uselessly) reflecting on our misfortunes, but resolve "to indulge us in our wishes. We four brothers can no "longer endure this treatment; our hearts can no "longer brook the conduct of these people. Death, "under such circumstances, is preferable to life. In "short, it is our intention to attack these Hollanders, "and we now make the earnest request that our father "will sanction the attempt by his approbation."—"My "sons," said *Kei Damáng*, "do not allow yourselves to "take this our situation too much to heart. If we "should be carried to *Bantam*, the sultan will protect "us;

* There was some indiscretion, on the part of the captain, in allowing himself to be drawn into this conversation, but the well-timed present of a delicacy may have thrown him off his guard.

"us; if to Batavia, we shall have the assistance of the "Malays;* or if to *Samārang*, I shall experience the "good offices of the Edele heer (M. Sambirik)." It is "all true as our father says," replied the sons, "pro- "vided they carry us to *Bantam*, to Batavia, or to "*Samārang*; but if they should transport us to *Pūlo* "*Damar*,† who will there afford us protection? The "employment of us four brothers will there be to twist "cordage for the Dutch; and God knows what sort of "burthen they may think proper to lay upon our father's "shoulders. Of the remainder of our brothers and "sisters they may perhaps make slaves. At all events "the property of which you have been plundered will "never be restored to you. Even with respect to your "life, there is no saying how long you shall be permitted "to enjoy it, and we may be doomed to lament your "death. But we entreat of our father to give us the "permission we have required. If we must be carried "off by these Hollanders, it is better it should be as "dead corpses, than to drag out in misery the remainder "of our existence in this world." *Kei Damáng*, after listening attentively to this speech, remained for a short time

* It is customary in the European settlements to appoint native chiefs to regulate the internal police of each class of people under their government, who are styled *captains*. The Chinese, Malays, *Būgis*, and others, have each their responsible chief under this title.

† An island lying off Batavia roads, called Edam by the Dutch. "The chief use they make of it," says Stavorinus, "is as a place of exile for criminals, who are employed in making of cordage; and over whom a ship's captain is placed as commandant."

time silent, being absorbed in thought. He then said:
" 'Tis well, my children : since such is your resolution,
" I recommend you to the protection of God and his
" prophet. But do not, my sons, place any reliance on
" my efforts; for I no longer possess vigour of body to
" grapple with an enemy."—" Were it even your wish,"
said *Nakhoda Lella*, " to join in the attack, we should
" not consent to it. You are now advanced in years, and
" were you to fall in the contest, it is not to be presumed
" that we could survive you ; but should it be God's will,
" on the other hand, that we four brothers perish, it is
" the more necessary that our father should live, in order
" to remove our sisters to whatever spot it may be his
" fate to inhabit. And although you should be the
" only survivor, still there are many friends who will be
" ready to assist our father." These words drew tears
from the old man's eyes, which he could not restrain.
He reflected on the probability that some of his sons
must be killed, or wounded at least, in the assault; for
the Dutch were strong and vigilant in their guard.
There were eight men in each relief: on the forecastle
were two men ; on each side of the after deck, near the
helm, two men ; and upon the poop, two men ; all
armed with musquets. In this manner were *Kei Damáng*
and his sons guarded. On shore, within the enclosure
of the house, there were, the captain of the vessel, a
serjeant, and twelve men, and in the Dutch guard-room,
a corporal and five men. All this force was to be
encountered by *Kei Damáng*, his sons, and his brothers.

Having

Having made up his mind to the enterprise, he recommended to his sons by all means to communicate their intentions to *Nakhoda Semporna* (their uncle); and accordingly when next he came on board with provisions, *Nakhoda Būjang* said to him: " What business, ' uncle, have you on your hands at present?"—" No " particular business," he replied; " excepting that I " have given instructions to (my brother) *Nakhoda* " *Darman*, to fit up a small vessel, to be in readiness " to follow you with a store of provisions and other " necessaries, to whatever place you may be conveyed."— " Do not," said *Nakhoda Lella*, " give yourself any " further trouble on this score, but exert your ingenuity " to furnish us with some weapons that will answer our " purpose, for we are determined to *run a-muck* (make " a desperate attack, at the imminent risk of our own " lives),* rather than suffer ourselves to be forced away " by these Hollanders. But even if we cannot procure " suitable weapons, we are still resolved at all hazards " to make the attempt with the best means in our power." *Nakhoda Semporna* having heard this resolution, returned on shore, and communicated the matter to *Nakhoda Darman*. " These four young men of ours," said he, " are determined to run a-muck, and their " father has consented and gives encouragement to it.

" By

---

* See the Malayan dictionary under the word أمق *âmuk*. The word rarely occurs in any other than the verbal form, مڠأمق *meng-amuk* ' to make a furious attack.'

" By what method shall we contrive to furnish them
" with weapons for their purpose?" *Nakhoda Darman*
immediately went to make a search and found four
siwars* fit for service. They then had a meeting of
the near connexions of *Kei Damáng* and themselves, in
order to settle a plan of attack on shore, as soon as
they could be assured, by the landing of the former, of
the successful issue of the operations on board. The
number of persons to whose knowledge this design was
intrusted was twelve.

About four o'clock in the afternoon *Nakhoda Darman*
came on board with a quantity of boiled rice, in a sort
of basket, and underneath this rice he had concealed the
four *siwars*. As soon as he appeared on deck, *Nakhoda
Lella* stepped forward to receive the basket from him,
when the former intimated to him that there were weapons
in it. He hastily carried it down to his brothers, and they
immediately began to eat the rice out of the basket.
The Dutchmen did not say any thing, but seemed to
look with surprise at the manner in which they devoured
their food, like persons who had fasted for several days.
Having finished the rice they put the basket aside, and
Nakhoda Darman returned to the shore. At night he
stationed a *sampan*, with two men in it, for the purpose
of keeping a look-out. The signals agreed upon between
the different parties were, that if a light should be seen
from the vessel, it was to be considered as a token that
all

* A weapon of the *kris* or dagger kind, having a small, one-edged blade.

all was well on board. If a firing of musquets should be heard, the party on shore were instantly to commence their attack on the Dutch who were there, to prevent them from lending assistance to those in the ketch.

Kei Damáng and his sons had been confined on board six days and six nights, and on the seventh night it was that they rose upon the guard, about the third hour after midnight. The motive for deferring it till this late hour was, that the moon had shone bright, and the wind blew from an unfavourable quarter (set on shore). They were apprehensive that should any alarm be given to the Europeans in the town, it might preclude the possibility of their friends entering *Kei Damang's* house, and occasion the destruction of that part of the family that still remained in it. When the third hour arrived, the moon had disappeared, and the (land) wind began to blow, (which prevented any noise in the vessel from being heard on shore). Each of the four brothers provided himself with a *siwar*. On that night their father was in a different part from them; for which purpose application had been made to the corporal. His place, which was tolerable roomy, was on one side of the principal cabin (on deck), and in it were ranged up several spears, to the number of twenty, that were in fact his own property and had been taken out of his own house. Two Dutchmen stood sentinels over him in this situation. *Nakhoda Lella* said to his youngest brother, '*La-uddin*, " Go you to the assistance of your father, and dispatch " those two sentinels."—" It shall be done," said the

other

other, " but I will first accost them under some pretence." He accordingly went towards the place where his father lay, when one of the men called out to him, " What " business have you here?"—" I am come," said he " to look after my father, and to inquire whether he is " in want of betel, as he complained of being a little " indisposed to night." The sentinel said nothing further, and *'La-uddin*, after speaking a few words (to his father), went below again to where his brothers were, and having taken up his *siwar* and provided some betel, returned to his father's cabin. *Nakhoda Lella* went forwards, and *Nakhoda Būjang*, along with *Si-Bantan*, to the waist of the vessel, where the greatest number of the Dutchmen were collected. When *Nakhoda Lella* had been on the forecastle about half an hour, he stabbed those whom he found there. *Nakhoda Būjang* and *Si-Bantan* followed the example, and *'La-uddin,* with his father, dispatched the two men that guarded them. The weapon employed by *Kei Damáng* was a large Company's pistol, with which he struck one of the guards, and killed him. From this moment the brothers could no longer act upon any combined plan, but each individually was occupied in killing, wherever he could find victims. *Kei Damáng* took down the lances that were ranged in the cabin. Observing some Javans, of whom there were seven on board in the capacity of seamen, he called out to them : " If you chuse to take part with " the Dutchmen, attack my sons : or, if not, seek for " yourselves a place of security." They immediately

ran

ran up to the mizen-top; not being inclined to take part with the Dutch, but desirous of remaining neutral.

About an hour had been consumed in this work of death, when *Kei Damáng* called his sons together and said: " Come hither, my children all: your parent is " anxious to see your faces. Here, take each of you in " his hand one of these spears." Presently three of his sons came about him, and took each of them a spear. " But," said he, " where is *'La-uddin?*"—" I sent " him," answered *Nakhoda Lella*, " to the assistance " of my father; since which time we have not fallen " in with him." Upon hearing this *Kei Damáng* shed tears; supposing his son had been killed in the struggle. But *'La-uddin* was at this time at the head of the vessel, engaged in looking at four of the crew, who were suspended by ropes from the bowsprit: such was the object that attracted his attention; for he was at this period but a lad, and had not been accustomed to think seriously.* Upon hearing himself called, he ran with speed to his father; and all being now armed with spears, they went to search for any of the Europeans that remained alive, and such as they found they put to death; not suffering one to escape: all perished through the providence of Almighty God, who in his divine dispensation, did not, on this occasion, allow his faithful servants to experience any kind of injury whatever.

Nakhoda

* This person, it will appear, was the ultimate writer of the memoirs.

Nakhoda Lella now shewed a light,* and a *sampan* soon came alongside to take them on shore. *Nakhoda Bŭjang* was stepping into her for the purpose, but was kept back by his father. " You had better," said he " remain in the vessel. I and *Nakhoda Lella* will land, " but do you three guard our property on board the " ketch :† and let me recommend to you not to place " any trust in the seven Javans who are with you. " Until we have completely effected the business on " shore, do not you think of landing." He then took *Nakhoda Lella* with him, and they proceeded to the house of *Nakhoda Semporna,* where they found *Nakhoda Darman* and other persons, to the number of eight. " Come," said *Kei Damang,* " let us attack the " Hollanders who are now in my house." Upon hearing his voice and that of his son (it was still nearly dark), they immediately descended and set out together. Having entered the *kampong* (inclosed space) unperceived, *Nakhoda Semporna, Nakhoda Darman,* and *Serif-uddin,* went up into the house, where the captain, the serjeant, and one soldier then were; whom they instantly dispatched. As soon as the soldiers belonging to the guard who were below, heard the noise of a
scuffle

* In low latitudes the day does not break earlier than five o'clock, and this seems to have been about four.

† The reason for this distinction amongst the sons is not obvious. *Nakhoda Bŭjang* might have been better qualified for carrying off the vessel, in the event of a failure on shore; or, being the eldest son, the father did not chuse to expose to further risk the life of one who would become the protector of the family.

scuffle in the upper part of the house, they issued hastily from the place appropriated to them, with their musquets, drew up on the ground in front, and fired into the house. As soon as they had given their fire, the party with *Kei Damáng* and *Nakhoda Lella* rushed in upon them. Of these latter, one man was killed and two wounded, but all the Dutch soldiers were put to death. *Kei Damáng* then gave directions that the whole of the Malays belonging to the place should make an attack upon the guard-room, which was done; but upon entering it, no person was found there. Five men had made their escape. With the exception of these, all the Europeans were killed; by the blessing and through the assistance of God.

It was by this time broad day. *Kei Damáng* gave orders that all his property on board the ketch should be brought on shore, but the arms he directed to be put into a small praw, along with some articles belonging to the Malays: the quantity, however, that she could stow was trifling. All the merchandise belonging to himself and to the other traders, was left behind (at *Samangka*), together with all their trading praws, to the number of fifty, which at this season were laid up on shore. He remonstrated with the Malays on their intention of accompanying him (in his flight). " In my opinion," he said, " it would be more advisable for my friends to " remain where they are, and not think it necessary to " follow my fortunes: uncertain as I am at present " where I and my children may find an asylum. Per-
" haps

" haps we may be allowed to live within the jurisdiction
" of the English Company, and perhaps not. Why,
" my friends, should you involve yourselves in these
" difficulties?"—" We shall never," they answered,
" suffer you to go without us, satisfied as we are of
" your integrity respecting the affairs of the Company
" or of the sultan. We consider you as an injured and
" an oppressed man, who, whilst you were rendering
" them every service in your power, have been treated
" in such an unworthy manner by the Company."
When this conversation was at an end he wrote a letter
to the governor, Mynheer Poer, and another to the
sultan, the substance of which was as follows: " From
" *Kei Damáng Perwāsīdāna*, in the country of *Lam-*
" *pōng-Samangka*, to his honour the Governor and to
" his highness the Sultan :—Respecting the circum-
" stance of my quitting this place, together with all the
" Malays who have been settled here, the occasion is,
" our being no longer able to endure the conduct of
" the Hollanders towards us. Whether it was or was
" not by the orders of their superiors, I cannot tell;
" but I have been treated by them like a dog; all my
" effects have been pillaged, my house has been taken
" possession of, and I have myself been confined as a
" prisoner. I am not conscious of having incurred any
" debt either to the sultan or to the Company, even
" to the amount of the smallest coin; and during the
" whole time that I have been a sojourner in this land,
" I have never in any instance defrauded or injured
                                              " them.

" them. I now humbly acquaint them that I shall
" never again have the opportunity of paying my duty
" to the sultan or of appearing in the presence of the
" (representative of the) Company. I was some time
" since honoured by Governor S. with the gift of a
" double-barrel gun and a pair of double-barrel pistols,
" both of which I now deliver into the hands of *Agas*
" *Jamāli*, together with the Company's ketch; and all
" the praws belonging to the Malay traders we leave
" behind us; taking with us only such articles as may
" be conveyed by travellers on foot. I am yet undeter-
" mined with respect to the route we may pursue, but
" I shall resign myself with confidence to the direction
" of God, who knows the future destiny of his servants."
The letters being prepared, he put them also into the
hands of *Agas Jamāli*, the sultan's agent.

Three days and three nights had elapsed from the
time of the massacre, when *Kei Damáng* set out on his
journey for (the English settlement of) *Croee*, with all
the Malays, men, women, and children, great and small;
to the number of about four hundred souls. After
travelling three days they reached a place called *Benkūnat*,* from whence he wrote a letter and sent it to
Doctor Blankin, who at that period had (temporary)
charge

* A small factory subordinate to *Croee*, near the south-western extremity of the island, and not far across the isthmus, from the upper part
of Samangka bay. The progress of such an assemblage of people,
carrying with them whatever could be removed, must necessarily have
been very tedious.

charge of the residency of *Croee*. It was to the following effect: " *Kei Damáng* from *Samangka*, presents his
" respects to the chief of *Croee;* being desirous of
" passing onward to that place, he earnestly solicits his
" protection. The occasion of his making this request
" arises from a difference he has had with the Dutch
" Company. It is his wish to live under the flag of the
" English; but if that cannot be allowed him, he begs
" permission at least to pass through their districts, in
" his way to any country where he may afterwards
" settle." Having dispatched this letter, he suffered one day to elapse before he pursued his journey. In three days he received an answer from the chief of *Croee*, acquainting him that he might come on to that settlement, and remain there till the business could be submitted to the consideration of the Governor and Council of Bencoolen. The effect produced by this letter on the mind of *Kei Damáng* was like that which thirsty plants experience from the fall of rain. He continued his (slow) journey, and in seven days from the time of his leaving *Benkūnat*, reached *Croee*. Upon his arrival he waited on Mr. Blankin, accompanied by *Nakhoda Sembawa*, who was ensign (officer of the country-guard) at the place, and having paid the usual compliments, asked him his opinion whether he should have permission to remain under the protection of the English flag, or not. " The matter," said the chief, " shall be brought to a determination in this way: I " will write on the subject to the governor and council,
" and

"and you shall also address a letter to them." At this period Mr. Carter was governor, and the council consisted of Mr. Wyatt, Mr. Darval, Mr. Hay, Mr. Nairne, and Mr. Steuart,* who were then assembled at Bencoolen. The chief of *Croee's* letter to the Board advised it of the circumstance of *Kei Damáng's* arrival, with four hundred persons in company, and of his claiming the protection of the English flag, in consequence of his having cut off the Hollanders at *Samangka*, from whom he had received ill-treatment; and desired to be furnished with instructions for his conduct on the occasion. The letter from *Kei Damáng* was to the same effect; representing the oppression under which he had laboured, his own and his children's imprisonment, and the plunder of his property; that his spirit could not endure this ignominious treatment, which on his part was wholly unmerited; that with the assistance of God he had effectually resisted them; and that he now craved protection from the governor and council, with permission to live under the English flag.

Eight days after the dispatch of these letters, his son, *Nakhoda Lella*, was ordered to proceed to Bencoolen, in the small praw that had come round from *Samangka* to *Benkūnat*, where he embarked, and his voyage was completed two days after the delivery of the letters (forwarded

* In the original these names are sufficiently correct, but their order is transposed. The members respectively are here restored to their proper rank. The fact of their being collected at the presidency took place shortly before the expiration of Mr. Carter's government, in 1766.

warded over-land). He carried his vessel into the river of *Sillebar*, where he addressed himself to the people of (the village of) *Kandang*, requesting that some of them would accompany him to Bencoolen,* as he had matters to communicate to the governor and council, as well as to *Daiong (Marūpa)*, to the two *pañgerans*, and the four *dātūs*;† being sent by his father to solicit protection and assistance from those personages, in consequence of the family having been engaged in a quarrel with the Dutch Company. "Such," said he, "are my reasons "for troubling you. I know not but it may be my fate "to be put to death by order of the government, and "in this case I wish that you should be spectators of "my execution. My vessel, which I leave here, I beg "that you, my friends, will take care of for me; but "in case of my death, you will do with her what you "think proper." The *Kadang* people having listened to this address from *Nakhoda Lella*, consented to escort him, and seven persons accordingly set out in his train.‡ When they reached Fort Marlborough he went to the house of *Radin Si Nāka*,§ who was governor Carter's

orderly

* The name of Bencoolen is here, as elsewhere, used for the settlement of Fort Marlborough, distant from it about two miles. From *Kandang*, near the river of *Sillebar*, to the latter, is seven or eight miles.

† The first of these was captain or head man of the *Būgis* people from Celebes; the others, native chiefs and magistrates, composing what is termed the country government.

‡ The natives always walk in single files.

§ This person was the son of a king of *Madūra*, whose tragical and affecting history (casting a stain on the English character) is well related

orderly serjeant, and acquainted him that it was his desire to be introduced to the governor, having a message to deliver to him from his father *Kei Damáng* of *Samangka*. The officer said it was well, and directly proceeded to make his arrival known, and to ask permission for him to pay his respects. The governor sent back the serjeant with a message to *Nakhoda Lella*, desiring that he would come to him at four o'clock that afternoon, when he should have an audience; it being then but a little past noon, and near his hour of dining. Upon receiving this message he retired to a house in the bazár of Marlborough, and at the time appointed, repaired to the government-house. Preparatory to his approach the governor had sent an order into the fort, to furnish a corporal's guard of eight men, and as soon as these were drawn up in rank behind him, he gave directions that *Nakhoda Lella* should be admitted to the council-room. After the usual compliments, the governor inquired of him from whence he came. " I " am come," said he, " from *Samangka*, and wait upon " you by desire of my father."—" What is the nature " of your business? Let me understand it."—" The

" occasion,

in a work entitled ' A Voyage to the East-Indies in 1747 and 1748,' published in 1762. " The old king," it says, " loved; the English, and " had his youngest son, at that very time at Bencoolen, for his educa- " tion; and as he wanted to cultivate a good understanding with them, " he ordered his son to dress and to live after their manner." This son, when an elderly man, was well known to the translator, between the years 1771 and 1779. He was no longer employed in a military capacity, and had wisely relinquished the European dress. His manners were polished, and his mind well-informed.

"occasion, Sir, of our intruding upon you is, that having suffered oppression from the Dutch at that place, we were driven to rise against them. In the contest they were all killed, and of the Malays on our side, two also fell. In consequence of this unhappy affair, all the Malays who were settled at *Samangka* have removed to *Croee*, where they wish to be indulged with permission to dwell under the protection of the flag of the English Company; humbly craving their lives at your hands."—" What," said the governor, " was the foundation of your quarrel? I am persuaded there must have been, on your parts, some cause (for strong measures), which it will be right in you to make me acquainted with, truly and without reserve."—" Sir," answered *Nakhoda Lella*, " I can inform you of every circumstance leading to it, from the beginning to the end, but the relation, I fear, will prove tedious to you."—" No matter," replied the governor, " for its prolixity. Begin and narrate your story at length, that I may be fully acquainted with it." *Nakhoda Lella* then proceeded to furnish governor Carter with a complete detail of all the circumstances that occurred, from the period of *Kei Damáng's* first settling at *Samangka* and being invested with authority there by the sultan and the governor of *Bantam*, to that of *Nakhoda Satīa* and *Nakhoda Dūgam* going to Bencoolen during the French warfare, for which he incurred a fine, and of Captain Forrest's touching at *Samangka:* in short, he apprised him of every event that had taken place. When the narrative was concluded the governor sent for Captain Forrest, and asked him whether it was true that he had been there some time since. " Certainly," answered the captain, " I did put in there."—" And what," said the governor, " was your motive for so doing ?"--" Because," said he, " I was in want of water and live stock."—" And " who supplied you with them?"—" A Malay chief, " who was named *Kei Damáng*, assisted me in procuring " whatever I stood in need of."—" Did you sell cloth " or opium, or did you purchase pepper there?"— " Whilst I was at *Samangka* I neither sold any goods " whatever, nor did I purchase pepper."—" Who is " that person?" said the governor, pointing to *Nakhoda Lella*. When Captain Forrest had looked at him, he said : " I know this man : he is the son of *Kei Damáng* " of *Samangka*. What can have brought him here?" — " He is come," said the governor, " to claim protection " from us; having killed the Dutch who were at that " place."—" The governor," said Captain Forrest, " will " do a just act in protecting them, for I am persuaded " they have not been to blame in the matter, but must " have been forced to it by the insufferable proceedings " of the Dutch. As to the idea that their debts might " have been a motive, it is by no means probable, nor " would thousands of dollars be an equivalent to them " for leaving their establishment at *Samangka*."

Nakhoda Lella was then desired to return to the bazár, to the house of serjeant *Miyūt*. After an interval of

seven days the governor again sent for him, to attend in the council-room, where the council was assembled, together with the two *pangerans*, and the *dātūs* of the town of Bencoolen, when he spoke to him to the following effect: " Return," said he, " to *Croee*, and convey to *Kei Da-*
" *máng* the letter that I shall deliver to you. With
" respect to the future residence of you *Samangka*
" people, you may settle wherever your inclination leads
" you. The place is to me indifferent. If at *Croee* I
" have no objection; or if you prefer coming on to
" Bencoolen, you are welcome so to do. Should any
" person sent by the Dutch government inquire about
" you, they shall be told it is no concern of ours, nor
" shall any information be given to them: but even
" if they should be acquainted to a certainty with
" the place of your asylum, you need not be under
" apprehension of our giving you up to them. The
" English Company is not accustomed to act in that
" manner, and you may rely upon their protection."*

Upon

---

* It is not incumbent on the translator to discuss the question of the justice or policy of affording protection to the leaders of this unfortunate colony, under the circumstances stated; but it may be observed that at this period, and ever since the formation of establishments by the English, in these parts, an underhand hostility had prevailed between the servants of the Dutch and English Companies, which manifested itself in constant reciprocity of ill offices. Our records in Sumatra were loaded with complaints of the Dutch undermining our trade, protecting our runaways, assisting our public enemies, occupying the settlements which these had taken from us and abandoned, and encouraging the natives to intercept and destroy our small trading craft—and there can be little doubt but that the records of Padang and Batavia teem with remonstrances and protests on

Upon receiving this assurance *Nakhoda Lella* lost no time in embarking for his return to *Croee;* where, upon his arrival, he was made acquainted with the death of his father, *Kei Damáng,* who did not live to hear the favourable contents of governor Carter's letter to him. He delivered it into the hands of his elder brother *Nakhoda Bŭjang.*

From the fatal hour in which they lost their revered father, it is not to be imagined what cares and troubles have been experienced by each individual of the children of *Kei Damáng ;* the consequence of having quitted their native land. The sons were separated and scattered over different countries, to which their fortunes happened to lead them. Some remained in the island of *Percha* (Sumatra), some went to the island of *Balli,* and some to those parts of Java that lie beyond the jurisdiction of the Dutch Company. These were their resting places. Like birds they directed their flight to wherever the trees of the forest presented them with edible fruit, and there they alighted. They were like chickens that had lost their tender and careful mother, who used to foster them. When it was their chance to meet with people who were inclined to shew them compassion, to those they devoted their services. Such has been the condition of *Kei Damáng's* children since their parent's death.*

For similar subjects: each of the parties supposing themselves to be in the right; whilst both were wrong.

* It would seem from these expressions that security for their lives, not countenance or encouragement, was the boon received from the

For the information of all respectable persons who may be desirous of knowing their (eventful) story, this narrative has been committed to writing, in a style of faithful simplicity, so that those who read it may think themselves eye-witnesses of the adventures of the family from *Samangka* to whom it relates. But God Almighty it is who alone knows what is good and what is evil for his servants in this world. Finis.

Transcribed on the eighth day of the twelfth month of the Mahometan year:* even at that time hath *Jurotulis*† *Inchī 'La-uddin*‡ made a transcript of the account of his own adventures and those of his family, at the settlement of *Palli*.§

Thus the poets say:—

[The poetry, however, is too rhapsodical, or sublime, to

English governor, whose answer may probably have amounted only to this: that their sanguinary quarrel with the Dutch authorities was no concern of his, and that the place where they should establish themselves was matter of indifference to him; with the important addition, however, that they should not, in any case, be given up by him to their enemies.

* The year itself is omitted, but being at the time of Mr. Hunning's residence, it was probably in 1788, or 1202 of the *hejrà*.

† *Munshī*, amanuensis, native writer.

‡ This name of '*La-uddin* is in the original لاءاودين, which may be presumed a Malayan corruption of the common Arabic name of علا الدين ' over or protecting the Faith.'

§ A small place about twenty miles north-west of the presidency, and subordinate to the residency of Laye.

to admit of an intelligible prose translation; but the purport of the first stanza is to insinuate, figuratively, that although the copy was recently made, at the desire of the gentleman who was then chief of the place (Mr. B. Hunnings), the work itself had been written long before. The remaining stanzas contain pious reflections and exhortations, mixed, in alternate couplets, with allusions to common objects, for the most part irrelevant to the matter.*]

* For an account of the *pantun* or proverbial sonnet, see the Malayan Grammar, p. 128 and 208.

THE END.

LIST OF WORKS
PUBLISHED BY THE ORIENTAL TRANSLATION COMMITTEE,
AND SOLD BY

J. MURRAY, Albemarle Street; and PARBURY, ALLEN, & Co.,
Leadenhall Street.

1.
THE TRAVELS OF IBN BATUTA,

Translated from the abridged Arabic Manuscript Copies preserved in the Public Library of Cambridge, with NOTES illustrative of the History, Geography, Botany, Antiquities, &c. occurring throughout the Work.

By the Rev. S. LEE, B.D., Professor of Arabic in the University of Cambridge, &c. &c.

In Quarto; price to Non-Subscribers, £1.

2.
MEMOIRS OF THE EMPEROR JAHANGUEIR,

Written by Himself, and translated from a Persian Manuscript,

By MAJOR DAVID PRICE, of the Bombay Army, &c. &c.

In Quarto; price to Non-Subscribers, 12s.

3.
THE TRAVELS OF MACARIUS, PATRIARCH OF ANTIOCH,

Written by his attendant Archdeacon, Paul of Aleppo, in Arabic. Part the First. Anatolia, Romelia, and Moldavia.

Translated by F. C. BELFOUR, Esq. A.M. Oxon, &c. &c.

In Quarto; price to Non-Subscribers, 10s.

4.
HAN KOONG TSEW, OR, THE SORROWS OF HAN.

A Chinese Tragedy, translated from the Original, with Notes, and a Specimen of the Chinese Text.

By JOHN FRANCIS DAVIS, F.R.S., &c.,

In Quarto; price to Non-Subscribers, 5s.

5.
HISTORY OF THE AFGHANS.

Translated from the Persian of Neamet Ullah. Part I.

By BERNHARD DORN. Ph.D., &c.

In Quarto; price to Non-Subscribers, 14s.

6.
THE FORTUNATE UNION.

A Romance, translated from the Chinese Original, with Notes and Illustrations; to which is added, a Chinese Tragedy.
By JOHN FRANCIS DAVIS, F.R.S., &c.
Two Vols. 8vo. ; price to Non-Subscribers, 16s.

7.
YAKKUN NATTANNAWA.

A Cingalese Poem, descriptive of the Ceylon System of Demonology; to which is appended, the Practices of a Capua or Devil Priest, as described by a Budhist: and KOLAN NATTANNAWA, a Cingalese Poem, descriptive of the Characters assumed by Natives of Ceylon in a Masquerade.
Illustrated with Plates from Cingalese Designs.
Translated by JOHN CALLAWAY, late Missionary in Ceylon.
In Octavo; Price to Non-Subscribers 8s.

8.
THE ADVENTURES OF HATIM TAÏ.

A Romance, translated from the Persian
By DUNCAN FORBES. A.M.
In Quarto; price to Non-Subscribers, 16s.

9.
THE LIFE OF SHEIKH MOHAMMED ALI HAZIN,

Written by Himself; translated from two Persian Manuscripts, and illustrated with Notes explanatory of the History, Poetry, Geography, &c. which therein occur.
By F. C. BELFOUR, M.A. Oxon, F.R.A.S, LL.D.
In Octavo; price to Non-Subscribers,

LIST OF WORKS IN THE PRESS.

The Travels of Evlia Effendi; translated by Herrn Von Hammer.
This work contains an account in Turkish, of the travels of Evlia in all parts of the Turkish empire, and in Turkestan, &c. in the middle of the seventeenth century.

The Tuhfat al Kebar of Kateb Chelebi al Marhoom: translated by James Mitchell, Esq.
This Turkish History contains a detailed account of the maritime wars of the Turks in the Mediterranean and Black Seas, and on the Danube, &c. from the foundation of their empire in Europe to the commencement of 1640.

The History of Vartan, King of Armenia; translated by Professor Neumann.
This work contains an account of the religious wars between the Persians and Armenians in the sixth century, and many important documents relating to the religion of Zoroaster. It is written in the purest classical Armenian by Elisæus, who was an eye-witness of many of the events he relates.

The Mukhtasar fi hisāb el-jebr wa'l mokābeleh, by Mohammed ben Musa of Khovaresm; translated by Dr. F. A. Rosen.

This is the earliest system of Algebra extant in Arabic.

The Tuzzuk Timuri; translated by Major Charles Stewart.

This work contains an account of the first forty-seven years of the life of Tamerlane, written by himself in the Jagatean Toorki language, and translated into Persian by Abu taleb Husseyni.

LIST OF TRANSLATIONS PREPARING FOR PUBLICATION.

Class 1st.—THEOLOGY, ETHICS, and METAPHYSICS.

The Sánc'hya Cáricá; translated by Henry Thomas Colebrooke, Esq.

This Sanscrit work contains the principles of the Sánc'hya System of Metaphysical Philosophy, in seventy-two stanzas.

The Akhlak-e-Naseri of Naser-ud-Din of Tus in Bucharia; translated by the Rev. H. G. Keene, A.M.

This Persian system of Ethics is an elaborate composition, formed on Greek models, and is very highly esteemed in Persia.

A Collation of the Syriac MSS. of the New Testament, both Nestorian and Jacobite, that are accessible in England, by the Rev. Professor Lee.

This collation will include the various readings of the Syriac MSS. of the New Testament, in the British Museum, and the Libraries at Oxford, Cambridge, &c.

The Didascalia, or Apostolical Constitutions of the Abyssinian Church; translated by T. P. Platt, Esq. A.M.

This ancient Ethiopic work is unknown in Europe, and contains many very curious opinions.

Class 2d.—HISTORY, GEOGRAPHY, and TRAVELS.

The Siar Motaakhkherin, of Seyyid Gholâm Hosein Khân; translated by F. C. Belfour, Esq., LL.D.

This celebrated Persan work comprises the annals of Hindôstân from the time of Timôr Leng to the administration of Warren Hastings in Bengal.

The Travels of Macarius, Patriarch of Antioch, written by his attendant Archdeacon, Paul of Aleppo; translated by F. C. Belfour, Esq., LL.D. Part II.

This Arabic Manuscript, which is of great rarity, describes the Patriarch's journey through Syria, Anatolia, Rumelia, Walachia, Moldavia, and Russia, between the years 1653 and 1660 of the Christian Æra.

Sheref Nameh; translated by Professor Charmoy.

This is a Persian History of the Dynasties which have governed in Kurdistan, written by Sheref Ibn Shems ud Din, at the close of the sixteenth century.

The History of Mazenderan and Tabaristan; translated by Professor Charmoy.

This is a Persian history of part of the Persian empire, written by Zaher ud Din, and comes down to A.D. 1475.

The Tareki Afghan; translated by Dr. Bernhard Dorn. Part II.

This is a Persian history of the Afghans, who claim to be descended from the Jews. It will be accompanied by an account of the Afghan tribes.

The Annals of Elias, Metropolitan of Nisibis; translated by the Rev. Josiah Forshall, A.M.

This Syriac Chronicle contains chronological tables of the principal dynasties of the world, brief memoirs of the Patriarchs of the Nestorian church, and notices of the most remarkable events in the East, from the birth of our Saviour to the beginning of the eleventh century.

The Ghazavati Bosnah; translated by Charles Frazer, Esq.

This Turkish work was written by Omar Effendi, a native of Bosnia, and contains the history of the wars in that province between the Turks and Austrians, from 1736 to 1739.

Ibn Haukul's Geography; translated by Professor Hamaker.

This Arabic work was compiled in the tenth century by a celebrated Mohammedan Traveller, and is not the same as the Oriental Geography of Ebn Haukal that was translated by Sir William Ouseley.

Naima's Annals ; translated by the Rev. Dr. Henderson.
This Turkish History comprises the period between 1622 and 1692, and includes accounts of the Turkish invasion of Germany, the sieges of Buda, Vienna, &c.

The Asseba as Syar of Syed Muhammed Reza ; translated by Mirza Alexander Kazem Beg.
This is a Turkish History of the Khans of the Crimea, written about A.D. 1740, and contains many interesting particulars relating to Turkey, Russia, Poland, and Germany.

Nipon u dai itsi ran ; translated by Monsieur Jules de Klaproth.
This Japanese work contains the History of the Dairis or Ecclesiastical Emperors of Japan from the year 660 Ante Christum.

A Description of Tibet ; translated by Monsieur Jules de Klaproth.
This will consist of extracts from various Chinese and Mandchu works, forming a complete account of Tibet, and of the Buddhic religion, of which it is the principal seat.

Ibn Khaldun's History of the Berbers ; translated by the Rev. Professor Lee.
This is a rare and valuable Arabic work, containing an account of the origin, progress, and decline of the dynasties which governed the northern coast of Africa.

The great Geographical Work of Idrisi ; translated by the Rev. G. C. Renouard, B.D.
This Arabic work was written A.D. 1153, to illustrate a large silver globe made for Roger, King of Sicily, and is divided into the seven climates described by the Greek geographers.

Makrisi's Khîtat, or History and Statistics of Egypt ; translated by Abraham Salamé, Esq.
This Arabic work includes accounts of the conquest of Egypt by the Caliphs, A.D. 640 ; and of the cities, rivers, ancient and modern inhabitants of Egypt, &c.

Part of Mirkhond's Ruzet-al-Suffa ; translated by David Shea, Esq.
The part of this Persian work selected for publication is that which contains the History of Persia from Kaiomurs to the death of Alexander the Great.

Class 3d.—BIBLIOGRAPHY, BELLES-LETTRES, and BIOGRAPHY.

Haji Khalfa's Bibliographical Dictionary ; translated by Herrn Gustavus Flügel.
This valuable Arabic work was written by the celebrated Kateb Chelebi al Marhoom, and contains accounts of above 13,000 Arabic, Persian, and Turkish works, arranged alphabetically.

Heft Peiker, an historical Romance of Behrám Gúr ; translated by the Right Hon. Sir Gore Ouseley, Bart.
From the Persian of Nizāmi of Ganjah, containing the romantic history of Behrâm, the Fifth of the Sassanian dynasty of Persian kings.

Meher va Mushteri ; translated by the Right Hon. Sir Gore Ouseley, Bart.
This Persian poem, of which an abridgment will be published, was composed by Muhammed Assár, and celebrates the friendship and adventures of Meher and Mushteri, the sons of King Shapur and his grand Vizier.

Ibn Khalikan's Lives of Illustrious Men : translated by Dr. F. A. Rosen.
This is an Arabic Biographical Dictionary, arranged alphabetically, of the most celebrated Arabian historians, poets, warriors, &c. who lived in the seven first centuries of the era of Mahommed, A.D. 600 to A.D. 1300.

The Bustan of Sadi ; translated by James Ross, Esq., A.M.
This is a much-admired Persian poem, consisting of Tales, &c. illustrative of moral duties.

Royal Asiatic Society's House,
14, *Grafton Street, Bond Street, London.*